ON THE POETRY OF
POPE

On the Poetry of
POPE

By

GEOFFREY TILLOTSON

SECOND EDITION

OXFORD
AT THE CLARENDON PRESS

Oxford University Press, Ely House, London W.1

GLASGOW NEW YORK TORONTO MELBOURNE WELLINGTON
CAPE TOWN SALISBURY IBADAN NAIROBI LUSAKA ADDIS ABABA
BOMBAY CALCUTTA MADRAS KARACHI LAHORE DACCA
KUALA LUMPUR HONG KONG TOKYO

FIRST EDITION 1938
SECOND EDITION 1950

REPRINTED LITHOGRAPHICALLY IN GREAT BRITAIN
1956, 1959, 1962, 1967

PREFACE TO THE
SECOND EDITION

On the Poetry of Pope, which has been out of print for more than a decade, is now reprinted with some of its more superficial imperfections removed—with misprints corrected, with a few changes of wording, with two short passages replaced by new ones.

I have only recently come to wish to see the book revived. Its revival, I had figured, would have to wait till the completion of a thorough revision. But the process of this revision, it is now clear, is making a new work which, when finished in a few years' time, will call for a new title. Meanwhile there seems enough interest in Pope's poetry to warrant the present edition.

G. T.

UNIVERSITY OF LONDON
BIRKBECK COLLEGE
19 *April* 1950

CONTENTS

CORRECTNESS

I. 'NATURE'

SELDOM has the *fiat* of an older poet fallen on more
attentive ears than Walsh's on Pope's. Pope told
Spence that

> About fifteen [i.e. 1703 or thereabouts], I got acquainted
> with Mr. Walsh. He used to encourage me much, and used
> to tell me, that there was one way left of excelling: for
> though we had several great poets, we never had any one
> great poet that was correct; and he desired me to make that
> my study and aim.[1]

On the face of it this advice appears suited to a prose
writer rather than to a poet. But for Pope and his
contemporaries the word *correctness* had the full
colour of novelty. The meaning Walsh gave it was
little older than Pope himself. According to the
O.E.D. the word had been first used in its new
sense by Dryden in the Prologue to *Aurengzebe*
(1676):

> What Verse can do, he has perform'd in this,
> Which he presumes the most correct of his.

Spence gives Walsh's statement a narrow interpretation:

> This, I suppose, first led Mr. Pope to turn his lines over
> and over again so often, which he continued to do till the
> last; and did it with surprising facility.

Spence considers the anecdote to refer simply to
versification, and no doubt this is what Walsh

[1] J. Spence, *Anecdotes*, ed. S. W. Singer (1820), 280.

principally intended. In Dryden the word had had
this connotation. Correctness, however, had, or came
to have, a more comprehensive meaning for Pope.

I

There were elements in this wider connotation
which inevitably had more impressiveness for Pope
and his contemporaries than for any later age, but
much of what Pope understood by correctness has
permanent validity since, in forming his principles,
he took over nothing that he did not find reasonable.
For Pope correctness was the newest term in that
Aristotelian body of doctrines which had grown to
such firm proportions in the work of sixteenth- and
seventeenth-century critics. Correctness freshened
the inevitable homage to Aristotle, gave the poet's
orthodoxy the self-respect of an original contribution,
the zest of not being entirely like his predecessors.
Aristotle had considered poetry as an imitation. But
the poet, he had counselled, must not simply copy
what he finds before him. His art must help nature
to realize the perfection, the grand simplicity,[1] which
she is aiming at but is always being accidentally
prevented from realizing. The poet must discover
the balked intentions of nature and so vicariously
free her. He must allow nature freedom to become
Nature. He will do this by removing all the acci-
dentals, by seeking the common ground in the mind
of all men (or of all men who can be thought

---

[1] A phrase adapted from Gray's letter to West, 16 Nov. 1739: 'I own
I have not, as yet, any where met with those grand and simple works of
Art, that are to amaze one, and whose sight one is to be the better for . . .'

of as having minds) and by erecting his poem on
that:

> First follow Nature, and your judgment frame
> By her just standard, which is still the same:
> Unerring NATURE, still divinely bright,
> One clear, unchang'd, and universal light,
> Life, force, and beauty, must to all impart,
> At once the source, and end, and test of Art.[1]

But, not unduly, the Renaissance critics felt nervous
about how this selection and idealization should be
accomplished. It was part of a natural humility
before the newly discovered or newly valued treasures
of antiquity:

with reference to what model or standard were they to select
in arriving at their ideal imitation? If they selected with
reference to an image of perfection in the mind, they invited
the reader or beholder likewise to look within in estimating
the justness of the imitation. But to do this would for the
neo-classicist be to lose himself in the vaguely subjective; it
would be to set up an inner rather than an outer norm, the
one thing above all he was trying to avoid. Why not get
around the whole difficulty, and at the same time show
proper humility, by foregoing the attempt to imitate Nature
directly, and imitating rather those great writers in whom the
voice of universal tradition tells us we find her idealized
image? Little need to go directly to nature, says Scaliger,
when we have in Virgil a second nature. The writer does
not need to chase an elusive image of perfection in his own
mind, but merely to copy Virgil; and the reader is also saved
the trouble of looking within, and has merely to compare
Virgil with the copy.[2]

---

[1] *Ess. on Crit.* 68 ff.
[2] Irving Babbitt, *The New Laokoon* (1910), 11–13.

The ancients had 'followed Nature' and so a later
poet with Nature as his aim would be wise to imitate
them: if he followed the ancient way of following
Nature, his own imitation of Nature would be more
likely to turn out satisfactory both for his own age
and for later ages. Virgil, indeed, had worked on
the same principle. He had found that to imitate
Homer was the same thing as to imitate nature:

> Nature and Homer were, he found, the same.[1]

If Virgil had imitated Homer, to imitate either Virgil
or Homer seemed theoretically the same thing. In
reality the two things were very different. Pope said
as much in conversation with Spence:

> In speaking of comparisons upon an absurd and unnatural
> footing, he mentioned Virgil and Homer; Corneille and
> Racine; the little ivory statue of Polycletes and the Colossus.
> —Magis pares quam similes? [asks Spence]. 'Ay, that's it
> in one word.'[2]

To imitate not Homer but Virgil was more congenial
to the Renaissance poet since the dominating element
in the Renaissance was Latin. In English poetry it
is the poets of Rome who have most say till the purer
glory of Athens is discovered more fully in the mid-
eighteenth century and has its effect on the poetry of
Collins, Keats, and Shelley. When put beside Virgil,
Homer seemed too primitive for an age already
enchanting itself with the gilded profusion of the
baroque. Dryden, for instance, considers it a pity
that Homer lived too early to benefit by the Latin
poets' discovery of the 'turn'. And so *Haec omnia*

---

[1] *Ess. on Crit.* 135.   [2] Spence, *Anecdotes*, 9.

quae imiteris, habes apud alteram naturam, id est Virgilium.[1] For Berkeley, the young Pope is 'one who knows so well how to write like the old Latin poets'.[2]

The allegiance to the original and secondary ideas of imitation meant allegiance to certain correct literary forms, and Pope is often found writing in these forms. As a boy he had written a tragedy, stealing plentifully from the *Iliad*. An early epic, with Alcander, Prince of Rhodes, as hero, was written and destroyed. His published work begins, as Virgil's had begun, with *Pastorals*. 'My next work, after my Epic', he told Spence, 'was my Pastorals; so that I did exactly what Virgil says of himself [in his sixth Eclogue].'[3] After the *Pastorals* come translations from Ovid and Statius, the mock epic *Rape of the Lock*, and the *Dunciad*, the full-length translations of Homer, the Horatian essays and epistles. In the *Elegy to the Memory of an Unfortunate Lady* Pope writes a Roman elegy and *Eloisa to Abelard* is in the manner of the *Heroides*. Pope's allegiance to antiquity must not, however, be exaggerated. Pope, at bottom, is himself. He was not the man to place a pedantic interpretation on his correctness, his imitation. He imitates not only Romans but Chaucer, Donne, and several smaller English poets. He feels himself as free as the scarcely correct Dryden to angle where he chooses, and in many ways considers himself to be carrying on Dryden's work. He seeks and praises power, spiritedness, colour, whether in

[1] Scaliger, *Poetices*, III. iv.
[2] Letter to Pope, 1 May 1714. Printed by Pope in his *Letters*.
[3] Spence, *Anecdotes*, 278.

men or writings. He honours the brother of his friend Arbuthnot in these terms:

The spirit of Philanthropy, so long dead to our world, is revived in him: he is a philosopher all of fire; so warmly, nay so wildly in the right, that he forces all others about him to be so too, and draws them into his own Vortex. . . .[1]

The 'fire' of the great poets has never been more brilliantly defined than in Pope's *Preface* to his own fiery *Iliad*:

that unequal'd Fire and Rapture, which is so forcible in *Homer*, that no Man of a true Poetical Spirit is Master of himself while he reads him. What he writes is of the most animated Nature imaginable; every thing moves, every thing lives, and is put in Action. . . . Exact Disposition, just Thought, correct Elocution, polish'd Numbers, may have been found in a thousand; but this Poetical *Fire*, this *Vivida vis animi*, in a very few. Even in Works where all those are imperfect or neglected, this can over-power Criticism, and make us admire even while we dis-approve. Nay, where this appears, tho' attended with Absurdities, it brightens all the Rubbish about it, 'till we see nothing but its own Splendor. This *Fire* is discern'd in *Virgil*, but discern'd as thro' a Glass, reflected, and more shining than warm, but every where equal and constant: In *Lucan* and *Statius*, it bursts out in sudden, short, and interrupted Flashes: In *Milton*, it glows like a Furnace kept up to an uncommon Fierceness by the Force of Art: In *Shakespear*, it strikes before we are aware, like an acci-

---

[1] Letter to Digby, 1 Sept. 1722. My citations from Pope's correspondence are mainly drawn from the letters which he himself printed. I have taken them on their face value as Pope printed them since I believe this value to represent the truth—or one of several truths—though not always the fact. The text followed is that of Warburton's edition of 1753, which he considered the most correct.

dental Fire from Heaven: But in *Homer*, and in him only, it burns every where clearly, and every where irresistibly.[1]

One of Pope's terms of commendation is the newly invented 'romantic', and he plans poems which were to have been very wild.[2] For all his Palladian principles he can remark, in a ramshackle old country house, 'one vast arch'd window beautifully darken'd with divers scutcheons of painted glass: one shining pane in particular bears date 1286'.[3] In a letter to Addison he records how 'strangely divided' his mind is between 'losing [his] whole comprehension in the boundless space of Creation' and 'groveling . . . in the very centre of nonsense . . . this little instant of our life . . . (as Shakespear finely words it) is rounded with a sleep'.[4] He has a sense of the darkness which surrounds all human systems:

The highest gratification we receive here [on earth] from company is Mirth, which at the best is but a fluttering unquiet motion, that beats about the breast for a few moments, and after leaves it void and empty. . . . What we here call science and study, are little better: the greater number of arts to which we apply ourselves are mere groping in the dark. . . .[5]

He writes, and helps to write, indecent poetry and prose which offends the serious ideal of correctness, but rightly insists, when the authorship becomes known, that there is a distinction between work and play.[6]

[1] Preface to *Iliad*, 1715, (folio ed.), B 1v-B2v.

[2] See below p. 43.

[3] Letter to the Duke of Buckingham probably from Stanton Harcourt, 1718.   [4] 14 Dec. 1713.

[5] Letter to Edward Blount, 10 Feb. 1715-16.

[6] Letter to Swift, 16 Feb. 1732-3.

The *Essay on Criticism* shows him abhorring the 'correctly cold', shows him ready to 'snatch a grace beyond the reach of art'.[1] He believes, then and always, that

> Some beauties yet no Precepts can declare,
> For there's a happiness as well as care. . . .[2]

And although this idea had occurred to earlier critics, Pope believes it with the force of his whole mind. He takes over the classic items in his creed with his eyes well open. He has his own intuitions about poetry and he knows that they must have first say.

The great secret how to write well, is to know thoroughly what one writes about, and not to be affected . . . to write naturally,[3]

and

Arts are taken from nature; and after a thousand vain efforts for improvements, are best when they return to their first simplicity.[4]

Wordsworth or anybody might have said the same thing. Indeed, there is little to fear for an author who borrows his rules for writing from the critics but whose standards for taking or rejecting are so right. Pope knew his own powers. He impressed so expert a judge as Dr. Johnson that 'it was [his] felicity to rate himself at his real value.'[5] Aristotle and his interpreters (often wrong-headed) counted for less with the better poets of the seventeenth and eighteenth centuries than with the less

---

[1] *Ess. on Crit.* 240 and 153.   [2] Id. 141–2.
[3] Spence, *Anecdotes*, 291.   [4] Id. 11–12.
[5] *Lives of the Poets*, ed. G. Birkbeck Hill, iii. 89.

good. The poets who were too pettily concerned
with keeping to the 'rules' were those who were
incapable of writing so as to 'tear [the] heart' with
pity and terror—the catharsis which Aristotle had
made the end of all those means he had observed
to be employed in the drama known to him. The
phrase just quoted is from the passage in the *Epistle
to Augustus* in which Pope considers it necessary to
state explicitly what the business of the dramatic
poet is.[1] The better poets followed their instincts
even though they put up a fashionable show of
conforming. They would have expressed themselves with little essential difference even if Aristotle
had never written, much less been interpreted and
misinterpreted. It was not so much the critics, for
instance, who governed the shaping of *Paradise Lost*,
but Milton who had read Homer, Virgil, and Dante.
The fine autobiographical openings of four of the
twelve books could be condemned by reference to
Aristotle's writing, though of course it is very doubt-
ful if Aristotle himself would have condemned them.
Pope writes in classic kinds when he does so write,
not because of critics but because of poets, and not
simply because of poets but because of his own
genius. If Virgil, Ovid, and Horace had never
written, Pope would have been virtually what he
was, though he might not so easily have found out
what he was. Although epic and tragedy were
theoretically the ideal goals of all great poets, Pope
has nothing to show in either kind. He recognized
that his genius lay elsewhere. He burns all traces

---

[1] lines 340 ff: quoted below p. 162.

of his youthful indiscretion in attempting them,
using excerpts from them later as illustrations for the
Peri Bathous.[1] Later in life he plans a blank verse
epic on Brutus but, like Dryden's projected epic on
King Arthur, it does not get written—to the satis-
faction of Joseph Warton and to the relief of Dr.
Johnson.[2] He translates Homer, but does not scruple,
any more than Dryden did, to make an original
poem of the translation. And although he imitates
frequently, he is always writing what he must. He
had always too much wildness, sensitiveness, 'happy
valiancy' about him as a poet to be dispirited by
having taken correctness for his aim. He merited
from the start Dr. Johnson's magnificent tribute,
a paean which does not lose sight of its subject:

. . . good sense alone is a sedate and quiescent quality, which
manages its possessions well, but does not increase them; it
collects few materials for its own operations, and preserves

[1] See Spence, 276–8, and G. Sherburn's *Early Career of Pope*, 84, note 3.
[2] *Essay on the Genius and Writings of Pope*, ed. 1806, i. 275–6; *Lives of
the Poets*, ed. G. Birkbeck Hill, iii. 188. Pope's plan for the poem exists
in Brit. Mus. MS. Egerton 1950, fol. 4 ff. Eight lines survive intact and
were printed (imperfectly) by Snyder, *Journal of English and Germanic
Philology*, xviii. 583, from fol. 6r of the same MS. Apparently they form
the opening of the poem:

The Patient Chief, who lab'ring long, arrivd
On Britains [Coast *deleted*] Shore [*written above with a dash preceding*]
   and brought with fav'ring Gods
Arts Arms & Honour to her Ancient Sons:
Daughter of Memory! [instructive Muse *deleted*] from [elder *deleted*]
   Time [*last three words written above*]
Recall; and me, wth Britains Glory fird,
Me, far from meaner Care or meaner Song,
Snatch to thy Holy Hill of spotless Bay,
My Countrys Poet, to record her Fame.
The three remaining lines are mutilated, the paper being torn across.

safety, but never gains supremacy. Pope had likewise genius; a mind active, ambitious, and adventurous, always investigating, always aspiring; in its widest searches still longing to go forward, in its highest flights still wishing to be higher; always imagining something greater than it knows, always endeavouring more than it can do.[1]

Pope is himself. He is also of his own time. But he is nevertheless half a Roman poet. His profoundest kinship is with Virgil. After Virgil came Ovid and Horace. Pope feels as they felt. He feels sometimes also as their successors—Statius and Lucan—felt. (To the end he persisted in ranking Statius next to Virgil among the Roman poets.)[2] These Romans deepen his melancholy, his tenderness. They help him in his search for what may be accounted beautiful and for the substance of the good life, as he saw that the statues of the ancients had helped Jervas to his 'beautiful and noble ideas'.[3] The Roman poets deepen his mood and strengthen his sense of what is worthy. They help him to form his critical standards of poetry. George Moore considered that the work of Jane Austen would have been thoroughly intelligible to Virgil and his fellows:

if the great dead were to reawaken, the Austen wine might be offered to Virgil, Catullus, Horace, Longus, Apuleius and Petronius Arbiter without fear that they would run to the window to puke, making wry faces.[4]

The same can be said of Pope. Indeed, he may be considered as working with something like that criterion

---

[1] *Lives of the Poets*, ed. G. Birkbeck Hill, iii. 217.
[2] See Spence, *Anecdotes*, 274 and 279.
[3] Letter to Jervas, 29 Nov. 1716.
[4] *Avowals*, ed. 1924, 35.

in view. His work satisfies his own standards of Nature.

II

This may be seen clearly in his erotic poems. His master for these poems is not Donne; his masters are Ovid and the poets of the Silver Age whose sense of pathos softened so many rugged places in their epics. In the Horatian *Essay on Criticism* Pope had dealt severely with the metaphysical poets and their 'glitt'ring thoughts struck out in ev'ry line', their 'glaring chaos and wild heap of wit', since

> True wit is Nature to advantage dress'd,
> What oft was thought, but ne'er so well express'd.[1]

Horace opened his *Ars Poetica* by laughing at a picture which mixed together several incongruous objects—his test of bad art is always the social one of whether or not it prompts scornful laughter. Pope might dally with such a style himself, but only for his own amusement or that of his friend:

> If I knew how to entertain you thro' the rest of this paper, it should be spotted and diversified with conceits all over; you should be put out of breath with laughter at each sentence, and pause at each period, to look back over how much wit you have pass'd. . . .[2]

Pope's views on the metaphysical style are those of Dryden and are, later, those of Dr. Johnson. In congratulating the Earl of Dorset on his love poems, Dryden had shown up Donne as academic rather than amorous:

He affects the metaphysics, not only in his satires, but in

---

[1] lines 290–8.   [2] Letter to Digby, 31 Mar. 1718.

his amorous verses, where nature only should reign; and perplexes the minds of the fair sex with nice speculations of philosophy, when he should engage their hearts, and entertain them with the softnesses of love.[1]

Pope's position had been stated at length and with spirit and perception by his friend Walsh in the preface to the anonymous *Letters and Poems, Amorous and Gallant* (1692). The passage is worth quoting at length:[2]

Those who are conversant with the Writings of the Antients, will observe a great difference between what they, and the Moderns have publish'd upon this Subject [love]. The occasions upon which the Poems of the former are written, are such as happen to every Man almost that is in Love; and the Thoughts such, as are natural for every Man in love to think. The Moderns on the other hand have sought out for Occasions, that none meet with, but themselves; and fill their Verses with thoughts that are surprizing and glittering, but not tender, passionate, or natural to a Man in Love.

To judge which of these two are in the right; we ought to consider the end that People propose in writing Love-Verses: And that I take not to be the getting Fame or Admiration from the World, but the obtaining the Love of their Mistress;[3] and the best way I conceive to make her love you, is to convince her that you love her. Now this certainly is not to be

[1] 'Discourse concerning the Original and Progress of Satire', *Essays*, ed. Ker, ii. 19.

[2] Charles Gildon quotes it in his Epistle Dedicatory to David Crauford's *Ovidius Britannicus* (1703). Dr. Johnson considered the preface 'very judicious' (*Lives*, ed. G. Birkbeck Hill, i. 330).

[3] This is, of course, a naïve explanation, but the love poet certainly wants the world (including his mistress) to think that this is his aim. Drayton's sonnets, for instance, were criticized by Drummond for showing love for his Muse rather than for his mistress.

done by forc'd Conceits, far-fetch'd Similes, and shining Points; but by a true and lively Representation of the Pains and Thoughts attending such a Passion.

> *Si vis me flere, dolendum est :*
> *Primum ipsi tibi, tunc tua me infortunia laedent.*

I would assoon believe a Widow in great grief for her Husband, because I saw her dance a *Corant* about his Coffin, as believe a Man in Love with his Mistress for his writing such Verses, as some great Modern Wits have done upon theirs.

I am satisfied that *Catullus*, *Tibullus*, *Propertius*, and *Ovid*, were in love with their Mistresses, while they upbraid them, quarrel with them, threaten them, and forswear them; but I confess I cannot believe *Petrarch* in Love with his, when he writes conceits upon her Name, her Gloves, and the place of her Birth. I know it is natural for a Lover, in Transports of Jealousie, to treat his Mistress with all the Violence imaginable; but I cannot think it natural for a Man, who is much in Love, to amuse himself with such Trifles as the other. I am pleas'd with *Tibullus*, when he says, he could live in a Desart with his Mistress, where never any Humane Foot-steps[1] appear'd, because, I doubt not but he really thinks what he says; but I confess I can hardly forbear laughing when *Petrarch* tells us, he could live without any other sustenance than his Mistresses Looks. . . .

He tries to be scrupulously fair to seventeenth-century poets:

There are no Modern Writers, perhaps, who have succeeded better in Love-Verses than the *English*. . . . Never was there a more copious Fancy or greater reach of Wit, than what appears in Dr. *Donne*; nothing can be more gallant or gentile than the Poems of Mr. *Waller*; nothing more gay or sprightly than those of Sir *John Suckling*; and nothing fuller of Variety and Learning than Mr. *Cowley*'s.

---

[1] Corrected from 'Foost-steps'.

And yet what he most wants to see in a love poem is lacking:

However, it may be observ'd, that among all these, that Softness, Tenderness, and Violence of Passion, which the Ancients thought most proper for Love-Verses, is wanting...[1]

Pope attempts in *Eloisa to Abelard* to supply the lack, and writes the best Heroic Epistle since Ovid.

III

The contemporary esteem for ancient poetry led to a narrowing of the range of the emotions considered appropriate for display in poetry. In the equable light of the Roman poets, enthusiasm and rapture seemed the crackling of thorns under a pot. The emotions of serious poems, it was held, should not, like those of Donne's lyrics, be the emotions of a young man uttered seemingly in the very moments of passion. They should be more steady, more permanent, emotions which Virgil could have sympathized with and understood. More than any other English poets, Dryden, Pope, Johnson, and Gray voice the emotion of a weighty serious melancholy, varying in its degree and quality, of course, from poet to poet and from poem to poem. Pope in particular attains those moods in which pity is found trembling like a frightened dove or in which it moves over the mind like a slow dumb wave, a bulge of deep water. Spence and Martha Blount tell how Pope would weep over tender passages in the poets—and one must remember that weeping had not yet become a

[1] Sig. A3r–A5r.

fashion.[1] In his own poetry of this kind, the mood is preserved from sentimentality by the technical control, which is the evidence of a moral control. The versification never lets it sag. Pope may even seem to be smiling at the gilded facets of the words—it was part of the good breeding of the age to attend to the sparkles of filtered light in the deepest shadow. His voice may scarcely be discerned to tremble; the reader guesses at the weight of the emotions while he watches the unfolding screen of syllables. *The Elegy to the Memory of an Unfortunate Lady* is one instance, or the *Epistle to Robert, Earl of Oxford*, or lines such as these:

> Blest be the *Great!* for those they take away,
> And those they left me; for they left me GAY;
> Left me to see neglected Genius bloom,
> Neglected die, and tell it on his tomb:
> Of all thy blameless life the sole return
> My Verse, and QUEENSB'RY weeping o'er thy urn![2]

Pope's melancholy is perhaps the deepest of all the many layers in the satire.

IV

To follow Nature meant to provide 'the general' rather than 'the particular'. This provision is made in all Pope's work. His satires, of course, are brilliant with particulars since they are out to show the age its very 'form and pressure', but Pope in these poems maintains the general in his attitude, in the processes of the thought, in the mind behind the detail. Pope differs in this from Donne. Donne

[1] Spence, 260.   [2] *Epistle to Arbuthnot*, 255 ff.

extends the bounds of his readers' experience, Pope
makes his readers realize the quality of what they
have already experienced:

> Pope springs eternal in the human breast,
> What oft was thought but ne'er so well express'd.[1]

No man until Donne wrote saw lovers' absence as
like a pair of compasses. Absence for Eloisa provokes no discoveries of this individual kind. Pope
does provide discoveries for the reader but they are
discoveries made among the materials in his memory;
an example is the famous lines on Vice:

> Vice is a monster of so frightful mien,
> As, to be hated, needs but to be seen;
> Yet seen too oft, familiar with her face,
> We first endure, then pity, then embrace.[2]

Dr. Johnson's words on Gray's *Elegy* could apply
as well to Pope:

> The *Church-yard* abounds with images which find a
> mirrour in every mind, and with sentiments to which every
> bosom returns an echo. The four stanzas beginning 'Yet
> even these bones' are to me original: I have never seen the
> notions in any other place; yet he that reads them here
> persuades himself that he has always felt them.[3]

Like Gray, Pope gives final utterance to what oft was
thought and, besides this, enlarges the reader's
realization of material which has lain in his mind
'unthought', embryonic or unvalued. He was still
following Nature, that is, tracking her down.

---

[1] I owe this witticism to my brother Mr. Arthur Tillotson.
[2] *Ess. on Man*, ii. 217 ff.
[3] *Lives*, ed. G. Birkbeck Hill, iii. 441-2.

V

For most of the poets of the earlier eighteenth century Nature had a strictly human connotation. But man lived his life partly at least in a world of 'rocks and stones and trees' as well as in the world of himself and other men, and so this Nature included whatever of external nature was found relevant to man. Wordsworth, of course, mixed the human and the external in other proportions and, according to his tenets, Pope was deficient in allusions to this external nature. He withheld from Pope the title of great poet principally because of that deficiency.[1] In a letter to Dyce of 12 January 1829, Wordsworth wrote:

These three writers, Thomson, Collins, and Dyer, had more poetic imagination than any of their contemporaries, unless we reckon Chatterton as of that age. I do not name Pope, for he stands alone, as a man most highly gifted; but unluckily he took the plain when the heights were within his reach.

It is clear from this grouping that Wordsworth is thinking mainly of the poetic imagination as it is active in descriptions of external nature. He is

[1] I take Wordsworth as representative. His statements on Pope belong to that early nineteenth-century controversy on Pope's status as poet. The controversy is a muddle of vituperation, pedantry, and vital aesthetics, and represents the nearest thing English literature can show to a battle of poetic principles such as that which waged round Victor Hugo. Though Pope is the stated subject, the real question at issue is the nature of the true poet. The history of the controversy has been set out by J. J. van Rennes in his *Bowles, Byron and the Pope-Controversy* (1927). Joseph Warton, Johnson, and De Quincey—in the *Encyclopædia Britannica* (1837)—also contributed notably to the subject.

reverting to the position he took up in 1815, in the *Essay, Supplementary to the Preface* [of the *Lyrical Ballads*]:

Now, it is remarkable that, excepting the nocturnal *Reverie of Lady Winchelsea,* and a passage or two in the *Windsor Forest* of Pope, the poetry of the period intervening between the publication of the *Paradise Lost* and the *Seasons* does not contain a single new image of external nature.

These words are meant to provoke feeling rather than to provide strict truth. There had, of course, been plentiful exceptions to Wordsworth's dictum —Dryden, for instance, and Pope himself outside *Windsor Forest.* (Tennyson noted that 'Pope here and there has a real insight into Nature, for example about the spider, which

Feels at each thread and lives along the line.')[1]

And there had also been John Philips, Parnell, Gay, and minor poets such as Purney and William Diaper. But a great bulk of evidence remains to favour Wordsworth's view. Copious description of external nature was never very near to the heart of Dryden and Pope, Young, and the rest. On the other hand, in whatever ways the poets of the early nineteenth century differed from one another, they all found in external nature a great deal of their material.

Wordsworth regarded the poet as a 'man speaking to men'. By this he meant something like deep calling to deep, an angel speaking to fellow angels. But that call and speech would have seemed mad

[1] *Alfred Lord Tennyson A Memoir by his Son* (1897), ii. 286. The line quoted is *Essay on Man,* i. 218.

to the Augustans since what it was trying to com-
municate transcended the ordinary established limits
of man's mind, transcended Nature. Man was not an
angel. Living his life among men, he had not enough
use for sunsets, celandines, yew-trees, cuckoos,
eagles, to warrant the long contemplations on them
which Wordsworth wished to share with him. At
most such things could be little more than decorations. Wordsworth, as a poet, was not a man speaking to men so much as a visionary trying to open a
neglected door in the human mind, a door that the
eighteenth century tended to keep closed so as to
avoid the draughts. For Dryden, Pope, Young, and
Johnson, the poet was a man speaking to the other
members of a civilized society who resembled the
poet in all but poetic gifts. Pope considered that
his more intellectual poems were addressed to a
small group. He tells Caryll, for instance, that he
does not expect a second edition of the *Essay on
Criticism* (the first edition numbered a thousand
copies) since 'not One Gentleman in threescore even
of a Liberall Education can understand' it.[1] But
Pope's audience was usually larger than that—the
Rape of the Lock in its second form sold to the extent
of three thousand copies in four days.[2] Pope's
audience was limited only by the barrier of a 'Liberall
Education'. And that audience had been prepared
for him by preceding poets and writers who had
contributed particular elements in that liberal education—by Waller and Dryden, by the authors of the

[1] Letter of 19 July 1711.
[2] Letter to Caryll, 12 March 1714.

Miscellanies and, not least, by Congreve and Wycherley. Whereas, to some extent, Wordsworth had to create his audience, Pope found an audience waiting for what he could give. This addressing of the civilized man meant a special area of subject matter for poetry. For Pope and the rest, the proper study of mankind is man, that is, the permanent core of human nature which remains independent of all extravagance, local, physical, intellectual or religious. Whatever else they spoke of, it was with man as stated reference. Man was the centre, however wide the circle described by his stretched compass. But it was not often that man was found stretching his compass very much farther than the 'town', than the society of his fellows. The part played by external nature in the mind of civilized man is always relatively a small part, and this necessary restriction of interest gets mirrored in the poetry he is inspiring. There is therefore more of society in eighteenth-century poetry than of trees and 'lonely hills'.

The poets of the late seventeenth and early eighteenth centuries saw and valued the large freedom of landscape, though Dryden, like most men, found that his eye could only find continuous rest on what was green in it.[1] That large freedom they saw and valued but had little cause to use. The limb of the human compass was seldom wheeled widely enough to include it. If the compass did include it and it got into poetry, its powerfulness often shrank

---

[1] Cf. Mason, *English Garden* (1772), i. 422–3:
> For green is to the eye, what to the ear
> Is harmony, or to the smell the rose.

because of the correctness of the couplets which these poets were finding so perfect for their strictly human material. This shrinkage, however, is never found in Pope's descriptions. In his mature work a landscape will often be allotted only a single couplet, sometimes two. But the space of those twenty syllables has the appearance of infinity. There is no other poet who habitually catches so much in a small glass. The *Dunciad*, for instance, provides the following:

> Lo! where Maeotis sleeps, and hardly flows
> The freezing Tanais thro' a waste of snows[1]

> To Isles of fragrance, lily-silver'd vales,
> Diffusing languor in the panting gales . . .[2]

> So clouds, replenish'd from some bog below,
> Mount in dark volumes, and descend in snow.[3]

> As to soft gales top-heavy pines bow low
> Their heads, and lift them as they cease to blow[4]

> See, round the Poles where keener spangles shine,
> Where spices smoke beneath the burning Line.[5]

Or there is the line

> The sick'ning stars fade off th'ethereal plain.[6]

When poets like Thomson, Young, Dyer, and to a less extent John Philips, wanted to describe landscape or skyscape more often than their fellows, they were wise to break away from the couplet into blank verse. In any case they could not have used the couplet as Pope used it. Pope was never tempted to

---

[1] iii. 87–8.   [2] iv. 303–4.   [3] ii. 363–4.
[4] ii. 391–2.   [5] iii. 69–70.   [6] iv. 636.

break away from the couplet for any major work because he could make it do all that he wanted.

Pope is under no delusions about the splendour and beauty of the world. He lived almost all his young life in the country. He is a country poet for Gay:

> You, who the Sweets of Rural Life have known,
> Despise th'ungrateful Hurry of the Town . . .[1]

and Berkeley, who has just thanked Pope for the *Rape of the Lock*, sees him also as a country poet, though with a field which could be expanded:

Green fields and groves, flowery meadows and purling streams are no where in such perfection as in England: but if you would know lightsome days, warm suns, and blue skies, you must come to Italy: and to enable a man to describe rocks and precipices, it is absolutely necessary that he pass the Alps.[2]

Even when he went to live at Twickenham, he was still virtually living in the country. His eye was sharp. He had begun as early as 1713 to take lessons in painting from Jervas, and painting still further sharpened his eyes. 'I begin', he tells Gay, 'to discover beauties that were till now imperceptible to me' and though he amusingly instances the 'corner of an eye', the 'turn of a nose or ear, the smallest degree of light and shade on a cheek, or in a dimple', the quality of the phrasing shows that there is more than amorousness behind it.[3] There is much important evidence in the letters and in Spence's *Anecdotes*

---

[1] *Rural Sports*, 1713, ll. 1-2. And cf. *To Bernard Lintott*, 1712, 80-3.
[2] Letter of 1 May 1714, from Leghorn.
[3] Letter of 23 Aug. 1713.

of the completeness of Pope's aesthetic sense. He
notes, for instance, that small black and white landscape drawings can give no idea of 'beautiful country',
since they deprive it 'of the light and lustre of nature'.[1]
Writing to Jervas he says, 'I hope the Spring will
restore you to us, and with you all the beauties and
colours of nature.'[2]   These phrases are memorable
and an apposite illustration of W. P. Ker's remark:

. . . do not the advocates of the romantic revival, and
the return to Nature, sometimes speak as if no one in the
eighteenth century had ever looked from a height over open
country, as if the daedal earth had been treated for the time
somehow like Giotto's portrait of Dante in the Bargello at
Florence, its green, white and red made decent and uncom-
promising with a coat of chocolate?[3]

We find Pope mentioning 'a solitary walk by moon-
shine'.[4]   Or there is this extended description two
years later:

I came from Stonor . . . to Oxford the same night. Nothing
could have more of that Melancholy which once us'd to
please me, than that days journey: For after having passd
thro' my favorite Woods in the forest, with a thousand
Reveries of past pleasures; I rid over hanging hills, whose
tops were edgd with groves, & whose feet water'd with
winding rivers, listening to the falls of Cataracts below, & the
murmuring of winds above. The gloomy Verdure of Stonor
succeeded to these, & then the Shades of the Evening overtook
me, the Moon rose in the clearest Sky I ever saw, by whose
solemn light I pac'd on slowly, without company, or any
interruption, to the range of my thoughts.   About a mile

---

[1] Letter to Caryll, 5 Dec. 1712.   [2] 29 Nov. 1716.
[3] *The Eighteenth Century* (*Collected Essays*, i. 78).
[4] Letter to Edward Blount, 10 Feb. 1715–16.

before I reachd Oxford, all the Night bells toll'd, in different notes; the Clocks of every College answerd one another; & told me, some in a deeper, some in a softer voice, that it was eleven a clock. . . .[1]

Torbay 'is a paradise', and 'summer . . . a kind of heaven, when we wander in a paradisaical scene among groves and gardens. . . .'[2] Autumn, 'the decay of the year', is

the best time . . . for a painter; there is more variety of colours in the leaves, the prospects begin to open, thro' the thinner woods, over the valleys; and thro' the high canopies of trees to the higher arch of heaven: the dews of the morning impearl every thorn, and scatter diamonds on the verdant mantle of the earth; the frosts are fresh and wholesome: what would you have? the Moon shines too, tho' not for Lovers these cold nights, but for Astronomers.[3]

This should be placed alongside Dr. Johnson's defence of the 'general' against the numbering of 'the different shades in the verdure of the forest'.[4] Pope sees landscape often, though not always, as a painter, but the point is that he is excited by it and interested in observing different effects. This element in his work—in both the prose and the poetry—has been neglected by other critics than Wordsworth. It is absurd, of course, that any poet worth the name should be thought of as blind to external nature and I should perhaps apologize for demonstrating the obvious.

[1] Letter to the Misses Blount, probably 1717: quoted by Sherburn, *Early Career of Pope*, 213.
[2] Letters to Edward Blount, 27 June 1723, and 13 Sept. 1725.
[3] Letter to Digby, 10 Oct. 1723.
[4] *Rasselas*, chap. x.

Spence records two *obiter dicta* of Pope which are of primary importance:

That Idea of the Picturesque, from the swan just gilded with the sun amidst the shade of a tree over the water [*on the Thames*].

A tree is a nobler object than a prince in his coronation robes.—Education leads us from the admiration of beauty in natural objects, to the admiration of artificial (or customary) excellence.—I don't doubt but that a thorough-bred lady might admire the stars, *because* they twinkle like so many candles at a birth-night.[1]

There are frequent descriptions of swans in English poetry—Spenser's stanza of linkèd syntax long drawn out in the *Prothalamion*, many small references in Keats, Wordsworth's

> The swan on still St. Mary's Lake
> Floats double, swan and shadow,[2]

Yeats's Leda poem[3]—but it does not seem that any poet has had Pope's luck or has troubled to look at a swan often enough to find it, rare almost as the phoenix, at a perfect moment. In the second passage Pope is found deploring the effects of the education which makes a thorough-bred lady invert the relative values of stars and indoor lighting. It was with this for theme that Wordsworth wrote the Lucy poem, 'Three years she grew. . .'. Pope is under no delusion about the beauty and splendour of external nature. He knows but has usually no reason for stating. As objects of beauty he prefers trees to coronation robes, stars to candelabra, but he has no description of a

---

[1] p. 11.   [2] *Yarrow Unvisited.*
[3] *Leda and the Swan.*

tree to put beside that of Belinda's exquisite petticoat; and the star to which he gave most attention
was the fictitious Ovidian one, the translated lock of
Belinda. The court decoration—

Bare the mean Heart that lurks beneath a *Star*—[1]

was of more value to his poetry than Hesperus, though
its vanity strikes him as the more wretched because
of the purity of Hesperus. Even in the superb line

The sick'ning stars fade off th'ethereal plain[2]

Pope is not thinking of an actual night, but of the
night in the mind of man when a curtain of intellectual darkness is being let fall. He is never for a
moment forgetting that man is his theme, and, since
civilized man spends the dark hours mostly under a
roof, it is sentimental to consider that stars have, in
the sum of life, more value for him than indoor
lighting.

Pope's theme becomes more and more that of man
in society. Perhaps by 1717 he was coming to see
that moral and satiric writing was his true bent. In
devoting himself to it more and more exclusively he
had the ancient authority which he coveted:

[The Ancients] constantly apply'd themselves not only to
that art, but to that single branch of an art, to which their
talent was most powerfully bent. . . .[3]

Pope's growing knowledge of his powers must
have been strengthened when the independent and

[1] *Im. of Hor.* Sat. ii. i. To Mr. Fortescue, 108.
[2] *Dunciad*, iv. 636.
[3] Preface to *Works* 1717.

vigorous Atterbury is so rapt with the 'Verses on Mr. Addison' that he writes:

Since you now therefore know where your real strength lies, I hope you will not suffer that talent to lie unemploy'd. . . .[1]

This limiting of subject excluded automatically the frequent allusion to trees and mountains. But civilized man must not be held deficient in sense of beauty because he did not seek to exercise it among mountains. Indeed, if the truth must be told, it may well have been the sharpness of that sense which decreed the abstention. If he excluded external nature from a large share of his attention, he was continuously aware, simply because of his civilization, of the works of man's hands. And, since this was the eighteenth century, that work was, almost automatically, beautiful in itself. Up to the nineteenth century, the product of, say, the silversmith was required to be beautiful. It was regarded at its proper worth, as embodying the aspiration, the schooled judgement of form and purpose, the skill, of one who was to metal something not unlike what the sonneteer was to words. The delight in the work of man's hands had been particularly strong at the Renaissance, when humanistic values stood high. It was included in Hamlet's paean on man: 'how infinite in faculty'. For the Elizabethans a term of high commendation is 'very artificial'.[2] This delight in the products of manual art lasts well into the

[1] Letter of 26 Feb. 1721.
[2] See, for example, the descriptions of pageants in Nichols's *Progresses*. In the passage on coronation robes quoted above the word has still its root meaning.

eighteenth century and finds its most perfect expression in Pope. It seems astonishing after the Chinese and Japanese, the Indians, the Persians, the Greeks and Romans, even after the clumsy fiery Elizabethans, that the work of man's hands in stone and metal should ever have missed receiving its full honour. Yet the Romantics seem to have preferred any accidental assemblage of 'natural objects'—even if the result of what the insurance companies would call an 'act of God'—to the art of man. Among them it was Keats alone who gave art its full due. His acknowledgement was the most handsome he could pay, since his aesthetic theory reached its most exalted expression in the *Ode to a Grecian Urn*. Wordsworth offers no exception. When he found that earth had not anything to show more fair than Westminster at early morning, he was still virtually among his Lakes—the architecture was only an abnormally small and still item in a sky-and-waterscape. And the same way architecture counts for little in *Tintern Abbey*. In the main the Romantic poets' ideal of beauty was provided by untouched external nature, and Keats is usually among them. Their sense of beauty is independent of a sense of form. Wordsworth seeks 'a something far more deeply interfused' among the bleak, magnificent or placid phenomena of the Lakes. Shelley is all for light and wind, Keats for colour and luxurious substance. But they seldom see how the materials provided by the earth can attain a perfection of form, and even of symbol, in the work of man's hands. Pope gives as much (or more) attention to considering such man-made beauty as to describing untouched external nature, and it is the exquisiteness of his sense of the possibilities of this kind of beauty that provokes some of his best descriptive satire. To step from his own deliberated house and garden—'All gardening is landscape painting'[1]—into the enormous pomp of Timon's proved intolerable. We know from Pope's statements to Spence that he required form from anything before he could pronounce it beautiful. From the tangle of materials out of which he made the descriptions in *Windsor Forest*, Pope selects only what he can place together in formal relationship—one landscape he found already half formalized for him by being isolated and inverted in reflecting water. But for Timon or his architectural deputy, form was attainable without deliberation, without the observance of the aesthetic proprieties. The elements of a proper and beautiful social arrangement may be discovered in the silver ceremonial at Hampton Court:

> For lo! the board with cups and spoons is crown'd,
> The berries crackle, and the mill turns round;
> On shining Altars of Japan they raise
> The silver lamp; the fiery spirits blaze:
> From silver spouts the grateful liquors glide,
> While China's earth receives the smoking tide.[2]

But Timon's coarse numerical bid for grandeur is excruciating:

> Greatness, with Timon, dwells in such a draught
> As brings all Brobdignag before your thought.

---

[1] Spence, 144. [2] *Rape of the Lock*, iii. 105 ff.

To compass this, his building is a Town,
His pond an Ocean, his parterre a Down:
Who but must laugh, the Master when he sees,
A puny insect, shiv'ring at a breeze!
Lo, what huge heaps of littleness around!
The whole, a labour'd Quarry above ground;
Two Cupids squirt before; a Lake behind
Improves the keenness of the Northern wind.
His Gardens next your admiration call,
On ev'ry side you look, behold the Wall!
No pleasing Intricacies intervene,
No artful wildness to perplex the scene;
Grove nods at grove, each Alley has a brother,
And half the platform just reflects the other.
The suff'ring eye inverted Nature sees,
Trees cut to Statues, Statues thick as trees;
With here a Fountain, never to be play'd;
And there a Summer-house, that knows no shade;
Here Amphitrite sails thro' myrtle bow'rs;
There Gladiators fight, or die, in flow'rs;
Un-water'd see the drooping sea-horse mourn,
And swallows roost in Nilus' dusty Urn.[1]

Pope's sense of beauty was more practical than that of Wordsworth. Not that Wordsworth's was impractical—a sunrise could certainly minister to a mind diseased or, if not that, to a mind unclean. But there are few whom life allows the opportunities for such a catharsis and meantime the mind remains smutted. There is more chance of the day's salvation if the cleansing comes from a stone urn in a garden, a carved portico or even the very cups and spoons: especially so, since such things are worthy of their

---

[1] *Mor. Ess.*, iv. *Of the Use of Riches.* To Burlington, 103 ff.

contact with the various light of Wordsworth's skies. The proportion of external nature in the theme of Pope's poetry is, more nearly than that in the poetry of most nineteenth century poets, the proportion in the life of normal human beings. The poet of Nature is too near the still sad, or the lively, music of humanity to be a nature-poet.

VI

'The life of a Wit is a warfare upon earth', wrote Pope in the preface to his collected *Works* of 1717.[1] It was in this long warfare that Pope would seem to have lost sight of his correct standards.

As a man Pope does not come up at all points to the ideal which readers elect for great authors. As early as 1712, Caryll had referred punningly to his 'Popish tricks',[2] and a man who is found once in clever subterfuge has all his actions suspected. In passing judgement on Pope's character, the nineteenth century went to the two extremes. At one extreme stands Byron. His mother's attitude to his lameness may have helped to sharpen his moral sympathy with Pope—his literary sympathy, of course, needed no sharpening. Byron will always receive the amazed gratitude of the 'friends of Pope' for his angry allusion to him as 'the most *faultless* of Poets, and almost of men'.[3] To balance this half a century later is the maniacal denigration of the Rev.

---

[1] Sig. a 1r.

[2] Replied to by Pope in his letter to Caryll of 21 Dec. 1712.

[3] In a letter to Murray, 4 Nov. 1820. *Letters and Journals*, ed. R. E. Prothero (1901), v. 109.

Whitwell Elwin. Scholarship, which partly means the getting at historical truth in minute particulars, may in time free Pope from much that has been laid to his charge, and form grounds for judging the rest. Scholarship is, indeed, already doing this. Professor Sherburn's *Early Career* has already shown that it is ridiculous to believe the worst of Pope. Mr. Norman Ault's researches in the canon of Pope's writings are incidentally contributing to the same conclusion. And in 1930, four years before Professor Sherburn's book, Miss Sitwell had already hit upon the reasonable attitude to Pope's character, mainly by the exercise of a vivid intuitive sympathy.

In judging the nature of Pope's personal satire one has to remember that it does not stand alone, that it exists in a thick context of abuse. Pope is not sharp, cruel, nasty and his fellow satirists gentle and clean. They are all as sharp, cruel, and nasty as they can be. And all of them, including Pope, write as well as they can, that is, make as much of their material as possible. Pope and the others always use against a man as much as they can find—truth or rumour about his person, character, history, habits. As an object of such abuse, Pope was exceptionally vulnerable. Never indeed has a satirist provided in his own person more obvious targets. Any urchin could, and probably did, ridicule his dwarfish, twisted body since, at that time, cripples still seemed comic, and even

Swift expires a driv'ler and a show.[1]

· With all this against him it is remarkable that Pope

---

[1] Johnson, *Vanity of Human Wishes*, 316.

became a satirist at all. It would have been much safer to have gone on writing stanzas on solitude, pastorals, lines on universal Nature. With all the obvious odds against him, he entered the warfare of the wits. Not enough has been made of his courage.

His enemies, of course, made the most of his physique. A fair instance of their manner would be Dennis's *Remarks on Mr. Pope's Rape of the Lock* (1728) which deliberately sets out to be temperate in abuse. Throughout this pamphlet Pope is referred to by phrases such as 'the Folly, the Pride, and the Petulancy of that little Gentleman *A. P—E*', 'the little facetious Gentleman', 'the only foul-mouth'd Fellow in *England*', 'a little conceited incorrigible Creature, that like the Frog in the Fable, swells and is angry because he is not allow'd to be as great as the Ox', 'this little Creature, who is as diminutive an Author as he is an Animal', 'a little Monster'. Pope must not be condemned because, like Swift, he uses the contemporary weapons.

It is worth noting that he makes the most of the faces of his victims. The lines on Dennis in the *Essay on Criticism* fix on his facial expression:

> But *Appius* reddens at each word you speak,
> And stares, tremendous, with a threat'ning eye,
> Like some fierce Tyrant in old tapestry.[1]

And there are the 'earnest eyes, and round unthinking face' of Sir Plume.[2] Pope's own face was of course the only unimpeachable item in his appearance.

Pope is sometimes found making the first attack, sometimes he was attacked first. Mr. Ault has made

[1] 585 ff.   [2] *Rape of the Lock*, iv. 125.

the plausible suggestion[1] that, since the lines on
Appius are seemingly based on personal observation,
Pope and Dennis may have met and, at that meeting,
Pope may have been angered, or even snubbed, by
Dennis. Dennis, that is, may have attacked him
first. Certainly Pope sometimes attacked first. Ned
Ward, for example, who had always respected Pope,[2]
found himself pilloried over again in the Dunciad.
But this treatment of Ward points criticism to adopt
a different standard. In Pope's eye a man, otherwise
inoffensive, might offend through his badness as a
writer. For Pope, a bad author was to literature what
a fool or a knave was to life. The Dunciad attacks
the denizens of Grub Street not as men first of all
but as authors. The poem, strictly speaking, was
not personal in origin. It was part of the programme
of the Scriblerus Club, the society formed by Arbuthnot, Swift, Parnell, Gay, and Pope to expose bad
writing and pedantry.[3] It is the cruellest satire of
its age only because Pope is the best writer.

But satire is not the only ingredient in Pope's
satires. Pope always constructs as well as destroys.
He always makes clear his moral position, and does
not stop till he has filled the eye with the spectacle
of virtue. Whatever people may think of his private
character—and of this there have been and are very
few who are qualified to have an opinion—that
character as it is revealed positively in the poetry is

[1] Prose Works of Alexander Pope (1936), i. xiii.
[2] I am indebted for this fact to Miss L. Herron.
[3] The best account of the origin and aim of the Dunciad is Professor
R. K. Root's Introduction to his facsimile of the Dunciad Variorum.

almost wholly admirable. Pope's sense of correctness (to put it no higher than that) would have made it impossible that it should not be so. Even if the reader considers that the torture of Pope's satire is often too exquisite to have come from a great human moralist, he must admit that satire of this kind is not the only satire in Pope, and that satire of this or any other kind is not the only moral poetry in Pope:

> Hence Satire rose, that just the medium hit,
> And heals with Morals what it hurts with Wit.[1]

The vicious or foolish characters are tortured, but the vice or folly is always measured against a proper, a 'correct' scale of human values, against a scale which Pope is always ready to state, to state precisely, and, as in the exciting fourth Epistle of the *Essay on Man*, to state at length. Indeed no other English poet (or letter-writer) puts and answers the question how to live with such sensitive and noble concern. The tone of this poetry (and this prose) must convince the reader that he is in the presence of one whose sense of virtue is as alert as the trembling, vivid eye one notes in his portraits.

Keats speaks of the 'snail-horn perception of beauty'. And Pope's perception of moral beauty, of moral depravity, and of all the subtleties compounded between them is a perception similarly tender. This is a quality rare indeed among satiric writers, and probably unique. There is certainly no other poet who combines the capacity exemplified in the character of Atticus with that exemplified, for

---

[1] *Im. of Hor.* Ep. II. i. To Augustus, 261–2.

instance, in Clarissa's speech opening Canto V of the
Rape of the Lock or in any of the verses to Martha
Blount:

> But, Madam, if the fates withstand, and you
> Are destin'd Hymen's willing Victim too;
> Trust not too much your now resistless charms,
> Those, Age or Sickness, soon or late disarms:
> Good humour only teaches charms to last,
> Still makes new conquests, and maintains the past;
> Love, rais'd on Beauty, will like that decay,
> Our hearts may bear its slender chain a day;
> As flow'ry bands in wantonness are worn,
> A morning's pleasure, and at ev'ning torn;
> This binds in ties more easy, yet more strong,
> The willing heart, and only holds it long.[1]

These poems are the most Virgilian poems of friendship in the language. And Pope's letters seem more
concerned with friendship than with any other
subject. He writes them usually 'in all friendly
laziness'.[2] He tells Swift:

Now as I love you better than most I have ever met with
in the world, and esteem you too the more, the longer I have
compared you with the rest of the world; so inevitably I write
to you more negligently, that is, more openly, and what all
but such as love one another will call writing worse.[3]

Friendship was powerful indeed if it could make one
write negligently who, like Ovid, had been born with
literary finger tips. And turning back to the poetry,
Pope is not simply the poet of Atossa or the references
to Lady Mary Wortley Montagu. If Sporus and

[1] *Epistle to Miss Blount, with the Works of Voiture,* 57 ff.
[2] Letter to Jervas, 14 Nov. 1716.
[3] Letter to Swift, 28 Nov. 1729.

Chartres are hated, Swift, Gay, Arbuthnot, Berkeley and Allen, are praised. If the *Dunciad* freezes the grimace on the face of Dullness it is because of Pope's regard for the 'bright countenance'[1] of intelligence. It is the conclusion of the *Dunciad* which most truly represents Pope's position, however much he has enjoyed the slime of the poetic games. Even by such simple tests his work is often noble. And in the most biting satiric analyses, pity may be as active as detestation. The character of Atticus hangs on a condition:

> Peace to all such! but were there One whose fires
> True Genius kindles, and fair Fame inspires. . . .

If there were such a one, who but must laugh—

> Who would not weep, if ATTICUS were he?

(And one must remember that Atticus does not represent the only verdict passed on Addison. There was also this, in commendation:

> . . . (excuse some Courtly stains)
> No whiter page than Addison remains.
> He, from the taste obscene reclaims our youth,
> And sets the Passions on the side of Truth,
> Forms the soft bosom with the gentlest art,
> And pours each human Virtue in the heart.[2])

William Cleland is not far from the truth when, in a letter to Gay, he defends the Essay 'Of Taste' (*Moral Essays* IV) and uses the words 'modest Epistle' and 'how tenderly these Follies are treated'.[3]

---

[1] Milton's phrase concerning truth in the autobiographical preface to Book II of *The Reason of Church Government*.

[2] *Im. of Horace*. Ep. II. i. To Augustus, 215 ff.

[3] 16 Dec. 1731. It does not matter for the present purpose whether or not Pope wrote this letter for him, or supervised it.

These qualities of tenderness and friendship were properly esteemed by one person at least in the nineteenth century. Hazlitt records how, in a dialogue with Ayrton, Lamb (who could read Pope 'over and over for ever') spoke particularly of Pope's compliments. His examples concluded with the 'list of his early friends' from the *Epistle to Arbuthnot*. Lamb recited 'with a slight hectic on his cheek and his eye glistening':

> But why then publish? *Granville* the polite,
> And knowing *Walsh*, would tell me I could write;
> Well-natur'd *Garth* inflam'd with early praise;
> And *Congreve* lov'd, and *Swift* endur'd my lays;
> The courtly *Talbot*, *Somers*, *Sheffield* read;
> Ev'n mitred *Rochester* would nod the head,
> And *St. John*'s self (great *Dryden*'s friends before)
> With open arms receiv'd one Poet more.
> Happy my studies, when by these approv'd!
> Happier their author, when by these belov'd!
> From these the world will judge of men and books,
> Not from the *Burnets*, *Oldmixons*, and *Cookes*.[1]

'Here his voice totally failed him, and throwing down the book, he said "Do you think I would not wish to have been friends with such a man as this?"'[2]

If such is the emotional response to a list of Pope's early friends, what can be said of that to the close of the *Epilogue to the Satires*?

> Ask you what Provocation I have had?
> The strong Antipathy of Good to Bad.

---

[1] 135 ff.
[2] *Of Persons One Would Wish to Have Seen*, Works, ed. P. P. Howe, xvii. 128.

When Truth or Virtue an Affront endures,
Th'Affront is mine, my friend, and should be yours.
Mine as a Foe profess'd to false Pretence,
Who think a Coxcomb's Honour like his Sense;
Mine, as a Friend to ev'ry worthy mind;
And mine as Man, who feel for all mankind.

His friend interrupts with:

You're strangely proud.

and Pope replies

So proud, I am no Slave:
So impudent, I own myself no Knave:
So odd, my Country's Ruin makes me grave.
Yes, I am proud; I must be proud to see
Men not afraid of God, afraid of me:
Safe from the Bar, the Pulpit, and the Throne,
Yet touch'd and sham'd by Ridicule alone.

O sacred weapon! left for Truth's defence,
Sole Dread of Folly, Vice and Insolence!
To all but Heav'n-directed hands deny'd,
The Muse may give thee, but the Gods must guide:
Rev'rent I touch thee! but with honest zeal,
To rouse the Watchmen of the public Weal;
To Virtue's work provoke the tardy Hall,
And goad the Prelate slumb'ring in his Stall.
Ye tinsel Insects! whom a Court maintains,
That count your Beauties only by your Stains,
Spin all your Cobwebs o'er the Eye of Day!
The Muse's wing shall brush you all away:
All his Grace preaches, all his Lordship sings,
All that makes Saints of Queens, and Gods of Kings,—
All, all but Truth, drops dead-born from the Press,
Like the last Gazette, or the last Address.[1]

[1] *Dialogue* ii. 197 ff.

Despite everything that the eighteenth and nine-teenth century found to dislike in Pope, one is left with a sense of this reverence for the sacredness of his weapon. Along with the torture there is all the poetry in praise of virtue, and, which is strange, the poetry of the praise is as magnificent as that of the detestation.

More than any other author Pope can create in the reader that brimming fullness of mood in face of what he shows as precious in human life, a mood both autumnal and vernal, solemn yet fertile, melan-choly and exalted. His imitation of the ancients led him to nothing more rare than this Virgilian fount of wisdom and tenderness. It is significant that the words 'language of his heart' come twice in his poetry, that Bolingbroke is praised for causing him to

> turn . . . the tuneful art
> From sounds to things, from fancy to the heart.[1]

The language of his heart was one that he spoke without taint of sentimentality. When he speaks it one is reminded of the similar experience afforded by Mozart's slow movements since in him, too, an exquisite regard for surface gives a masking decency and humility to the full emotions; and, moreover, in Mozart there is often a strictly ticking accompani-ment to the 'emotional' melody which finds its counterpart in the precision of Pope's versification. We see the chastened survivor of the tumult rather than the sufferer. It is a sadder and wiser spirit which is remembering. The reader is reverent, too. Hazlitt,

[1] *Ep. to Arbuthnot*, 399, *Im. of Hor.* Ep. II. i. To Augustus, 78, and *Essay on Man*, iv. 391–2.

the profoundest critic of the *Rape of the Lock* did not know whether to laugh or to weep over the poem. When Pope speaks seriously in his own person there is nothing in his language of what Keats called the egotistical sublime. It is un-Miltonic in its quietness. To withdraw in pride, to dwell apart like a star, would have offended the ideal of 'correctness'. When he did withdraw it was into final silence and unhappiness. The note appended to the *Epilogue*:

This was the last poem of the kind printed by our author, with a resolution to publish no more; but to enter thus, in the most plain and solemn manner he could, a sort of PROTEST against that insuperable corruption and depravity of manners, which he had been so unhappy as to live to see. Could he have hoped to have amended any, he had continued those attacks; but bad men were grown so shameless and so powerful, that Ridicule was become as unsafe as it was ineffectual. The Poem raised him, as he knew it would, some enemies; but he had reason to be satisfied with the approbation of good men, and the testimony of his own conscience.

There is no reason to consider these noble sentences as hypocritical. They represent a solemn moment for the eighteenth century, the closing down in long-deferred disillusion of a great critical intelligence, the most vigilant and subtle discriminator of intention and conduct in the whole gamut of our literature.

CORRECTNESS
II. DESIGN
I

Pope spoke to Spence of the 'three distinct *tours* in poetry: the design, the language, and the versification'.[1] He tried to achieve these in correct forms.

Pope told Spence that he had once intended to write a

Persian fable in which I should have given a full loose to description and imagination. It would have been a very wild thing.[2]

But this wild thing never got written, as Keats's *Endymion* did. Its wildness, like that of Dr. Johnson's *Fountains*, would have been restrained, no doubt, by the moral which, in a letter to Judith Cowper, Pope stated as an essential element in what seems to have been the same projected poem:

I have long had an inclination to tell a fairy tale, the more wild and exotic the better; therefore a *vision*, which is confined to no rules of probability, will take in all the variety and luxuriancy of description you will; provided there be an apparent moral to it. I think, one or two of the Persian tales would give one hints for such an invention. . . .[3]

In a way the *Iliad* may be thought of as Pope's very wild thing. Pope admired Homer for the 'Spirit and Fire which makes his chief Character',[4] and sees to it that the flames crackle spiritedly in his version. He

---

[1] p. 23.   [2] p. 140.
[3] 26 Sept. 1723.   [4] Preface, folio edition, K [1st series]1r.

could sooner 'pardon Frenzy than Frigidity' in a
translator,[1] a pardon which may be thought to be
invited by parts of his own version. To see how
Pope can toss the flames, one has only to compare
with the original the description of Vulcan's inter-
vention in Book XXI,[2] or the brilliantly onomatopoetic description of the felling of trees in Book XXIII:

> Loud sounds the Axe, redoubling Strokes on Strokes;
> On all sides round the Forest hurles her Oaks
> Headlong. Deep-echoing groan the Thickets brown;
> Then rustling, crackling, crashing, thunder down.[3]

And yet the Homer is exquisitely controlled. The
fire is never conflagration. And control is exquisite
again in *Eloisa to Abelard*, a poem of which Byron
wrote 'If you search for passion, where is it to be
found stronger?'[4] and which Porson would sing,
whether drunk or sober, from beginning to end.

Although Pope had as complex a sense of the
paragraph as any seventeenth-century rhetorician, he
cannot be said to have put into practice any very
complex idea of form, of design. He produced no
work so interrelated, for example, as *Measure for
Measure* or indeed any mature play of Shakespeare.
His idea of form was not that of the centre with its
nimbus of radiations, but that of growth along a line.
When he speaks of 'the whole' he does not always
mean more than this.

Pope seems to have noted three stages in the
history of a poem, the third of which could be sub-

---

[1] Preface, folio edition, H [*1st series*] 1[v].
[2] 398 ff.: the passage is quoted pp. 171 f., below.   [3] 144 ff.
[4] *Works: Letters and Journals*, ed. R. E. Prothero (1900) iv. 489.

divided indefinitely. The poet has his 'inspiration', the fiery condition of mind which can be counted on to give his work the quality of poetry. But he must keep the fire well under control or it will devastate his poem-on-paper, the designed whole—

> 'Tis more to guide, than spur the Muse's steed;
> Restrain his fury, than provoke his speed.[1]

The designing of the poem is the third stage, but the design must not be decided on till the poet has passed through an adequate period of consideration. During this consideration he is not so much imposing a design on his material as allowing the individual nature of that material to elect a design for itself. It was the same in poetry as in gardening:

> Consult the Genius of the Place in all[2]

and

In laying out a garden, the first thing to be considered is the genius of the place.[3]

After the 'genius' of his material had had its say, the poet effected the plan as simply as he could without being false to that 'genius'.

Pope was interested in the rules for the other arts, the rules in accordance with which they achieved structural unity. The following are extracts from his conversations with Spence:

. . . all the rules of architecture would be reducible to three or four heads. The justness of the openings, bearings upon bearings, and the regularity of the pillars.

[1] *Ess. on Crit.* 84 f.
[2] *Mor. Ess.* iv. *Of the Use of Riches.* To Burlington, 57.
[3] Spence, 12.

That which is not just in buildings, is disagreeable to the eye; (as a greater upon a slighter, &c.) This he called 'the reasoning of the eye'.[1]

All gardening is landscape painting. [This was spoken as we were looking upon the round of the physic garden at Oxford; and the view through it, that looks so much like a picture hung up.][2]

And he considered a 'love to parts'[3] as dangerous in criticism as in poetry.

In the *Essay on Criticism* a complete design is appraised during the counsel to the critic:

> A perfect Judge will read each work of Wit
> With the same spirit that its author writ:
> Survey the WHOLE . . .
>
> In wit, as nature, what affects our hearts
> Is not th' exactness of peculiar parts;
> 'Tis not a lip, or eye, we beauty call,
> But the joint force and full result of all. . . .[4]

The importance of design is implied between the lines which counsel the control of the imagination: the subject of good art is Nature and

> Art from that fund each just supply provides,
> Works without show, and without pomp presides:
> In some fair body thus th'informing soul
> With spirits feeds, with vigour fills the whole,
> Each motion guides, and ev'ry nerve sustains;
> Itself unseen, but in th'effects, remains.
> Some, to whom Heav'n in wit has been profuse,
> Want as much more, to turn it to its use;
> For wit and judgment often are at strife,
> Tho' meant each other's aid, like man and wife.[5]

[1] p. 12.   [2] pp. 144-5.   [3] *Essay on Crit.* 288.
[4] 233 ff.   [5] 74 ff.

In these last quotations Pope is praising the kind
of form which his poems did not often require. The
metaphor of the human body—which is Horace's
who had it of Aristotle who had it of Plato's *Phaedrus*
—shows form to be more than growth along a line
however much that line may curve. Pope's poems
seldom required this functional shapeliness of a
living organism. It is not so much as bodies that
one sees most of his designs. Rather they are plants
which grow from a beginning to an end, their stems
branching into leaves and flowers at what are felt to
be the proper intervals. The *Essay on Criticism* is
such a growth, though the flowers—in the shape of
similes—are perhaps too heavy for their stems. The
Essay on Criticism is more shapely than Horace's
Ars Poetica which is 'probably only fragments of
what he designed; it wants the regularity that flows
from the following a plan'.[1] *Eloisa to Abelard* pre-
sents a series of scenes and moods all about equal
in the number of their lines, one leading properly
into another, all of them arranged to fit the psycho-
logical progress of Eloisa's mind. Even small poems,
Pope held, should be written on a plan: 'this method
is evident in Tibullus, and Ovid's Elegies, and
almost all the pieces of the ancients'.[2] All Pope's
minor poems, often among his finest work, are as
perfect as those of his masters.

In the *Essay on Man* and the *Moral Essays* the
problems are the same. They are the same, too, in
the *Imitations of Horace* where Pope had Horace both
to help and hinder. The problems are those often of

[1] Spence, 1.   [2] Id.

the prose essay as Bacon wrote it. The nature of the essay or epistle was free but it required the horizontal continuity of an argument. Pope is sometimes considered to have been prevented by the defect of one of his virtues from achieving this continuity. The heroic couplet as used by him was not, it is said, the appropriate medium for the continuous development of an essay. But this view cannot stand. Pope mastered the use of the couplet for the purposes of argument as he mastered it for any other purpose for which he used it.

Each paragraph progresses at a regular pace or, if it accelerates, does so at a perfectly controlled rate. And the ligatures between paragraphs are of an Ovidian strength and neatness. Occasionally, as in the second of the two essays on riches, an anecdote may seem to be given disproportionate space. But here Pope would have sought refuge in Horace's example. Horace, on one occasion, gives up more than half his space to a single anecdote.[1] Spence shows Pope planning the structure of what later became known as the *Essay on Man*:

The first epistle is to be to the whole work, what a scale is to a book of maps; and in this, I reckon, lies my greatest difficulty: not only in settling and ranging the parts of it aright, but in making them agreeable enough to be read with pleasure.[2]

Pope was at his weakest as a philosopher. The *Essay on Man* is beautifully planned on paper, but not as reason.

The design of all these poems is what one might

---

[1] *Epistles*, i. 7.   [2] 16.

call perfect, though their kind of design is not the most difficult. The main difficulty in such poems is to make the transitions. The transition was a grace which the eighteenth century practised with care, taking Ovid as its master. Boileau considered the transition 'le plus difficile chef-d'œuvre de la poésie'.[1] But even the Grub Street essayists were adepts in the art:

Of all the pretty Arts in which our modern Writers excel, there is not any which is more to be recommended to the Imitation of Beginners, than the Skill of Transition from one Subject to another. I know not whether I make my self well understood; but it is certain, that the Way of stringing a Discourse, used in the *Mercury Gallant*, the *Gentleman's Journal*, and other learned Writings, not to mention how naturally Things present themselves to such as harangue in Pulpits, and other Occasions which occur to the Learned, are Methods worthy Commendation.[2]

All the poets practise it. It was the absence of transitions in the prose of Macpherson's Ossian which provided part of its startling novelty (though readers had been partly prepared for the shock by the blank verse of Glover's *Leonidas*). Blair in his dissertation on Ossian considered the lack of transitions as a mark of the primitive simplicity of the poet. Pope's transitions are masterly and various. As example one might take a passage at random: Belinda is on the point of winning the game of ombre:

An Ace of Hearts steps forth: The King unseen
Lurk'd in her hand, and mourn'd his captive Queen:

[1] Letter to Racine, 7 Oct. 1692.
[2] *Tatler*, No. 67.

He springs to Vengeance with an eager pace,
And falls like thunder on the prostrate Ace.
The nymph exulting fills with shouts the sky;
The walls, the woods, and long canals reply.

O thoughtless mortals! ever blind to fate,
Too soon dejected, and too soon elate.
Sudden, these honours shall be snatch'd away,
And curs'd for ever this victorious day.

For lo! the board with cups and spoons is crown'd,
The berries crackle, and the mill turns round;
On shining Altars of Japan they raise
The silver lamp; the fiery spirits blaze:
From silver spouts the grateful liquors glide,
While China's earth receives the smoking tide.
At once they gratify their scent and taste,
And frequent cups prolong the rich repast.
Straight hover round the Fair her airy band;
Some, as she sipp'd, the fuming liquor fann'd,
Some o'er her lap their careful plumes display'd,
Trembling, and conscious of the rich brocade.
Coffee, (which makes the politician wise,
And see thro' all things with his half-shut eyes)
Sent up in vapours to the Baron's brain
New Stratagems, the radiant Lock to gain.
Ah cease, rash youth! desist ere 'tis too late,
Fear the just Gods, and think of Scylla's Fate!
Chang'd to a bird, and sent to flit in air,
She dearly pays for Nisus' injur'd hair!

But when to mischief mortals bend their will,
How soon they find fit instruments of ill!
Just then, Clarissa drew with tempting grace
A two-edg'd weapon from her shining case:
So Ladies in Romance assist their Knight,
Present the spear, and arm him for the fight.

> He takes the gift with rev'rence, and extends
> The little engine on his fingers' ends;
> This just behind Belinda's neck he spread,
> As o'er the fragrant steams she bends her head.[1]

The transitions in this passage may be expanded as follows. Belinda's shout of triumph is sent echoing along the woods and waters of the Court. But the poet, wiser and sad himself, is already murmuring his fears:

> O thoughtless mortals! . . .

Those fears are only too much warranted—

> For lo! the board with cups and spoons is crown'd.

The scene is already unfolding itself, inevitably and with deceptive gaiety:

> The berries crackle, and the mill turns round. . . .

Belinda sips her coffee and the faithful sylphs are in attendance, cooling it for her lips, or ready to intercept any drop that may fall on her brocade. But the coffee acts as a stimulant on the Baron who, grim as a politician, finds new stratagems forming in his brain. The poet pleads with him, but uselessly since, of course, the devil is always at hand with means. In this instance, it is Clarissa who is just then—as if accidentally—drawing her scissors from their case. The Baron takes them and is already exercising his fingers on them.

The *Moral Essays* and *Imitation of Horace* show everywhere a consummate handling of transitions:

> Whether the Charmer sinner it, or saint it,
> If Folly grow romantic, I must paint it.

[1] *Rape of the Lock*, iii. 95 ff.

> Come then, the colours and the ground prepare!
> Dip in the Rainbow, trick her off in Air. . . .[1]

> But what are these to great Atossa's mind?[2]

> And swear, not ADDISON himself was safe.
>   Peace to all such! but were there One whose fires
> True Genius kindles, and fair Fame inspires. . . .[3]

These are typical examples of transitions which may be seen working in the syntax, with their *thens* and *buts*. Pope makes, of course, full use of such conjunctions. But his transitions often transcend the mechanical aids of syntax. They are often engineered through the sense alone, and it is in this more difficult kind of transition that Pope shows himself most a master. The modulation, often into a key which is technically remote but strongly related in emotion, sometimes take place without a vehicle, exactly as it does in Mozart's operas where the emotional line turns with a sharp corner instead of a curve, as if the preceding emotions have ended by pressing a switch and so have brought new forces into play. The *Guardian*, in a very interesting paper, had noted transitions of this kind:

. . . sometimes gentle Deviations, sometimes bold and even abrupt Digressions, where the Dignity of the Subject seems to give the Impulse, are Proofs of a noble Genius; as winding about and returning artfully to the main Design, are marks of Address and Dexterity.[4]

---

[1] *Mor. Essays*, ii. *Of the Characters of Women*, 15 ff.
[2] Id. 115.
[3] *Epistle to Arbuthnot*, 192 ff.
[4] No. 12.

I take the following examples:

> When Hopkins dies, a thousand lights attend
> The wretch, who living sav'd a candle's end:
> Should'ring God's altar a vile image stands,
> Belies his features, nay extends his hands;
> That live-long wig which Gorgon's self might own,
> Eternal buckle takes in Parian stone.
> Behold what blessings Wealth to life can lend!
> And see, what comfort it affords our end.
>   In the worst inn's worst room, with mat half-hung,
> The floors of plaister, and the walls of dung. . . .[1]

Or this—Pope has been speaking of his friends:

> From these the world will judge of men and books,
> Not from the *Burnets*, *Oldmixons*, and *Cookes*.
>   Soft were my numbers. . . .[2]

(Here the transition may be seen as much in the change from cacophony to euphony as in the sense.) Further examples are:

> A lash like mine no honest man shall dread,
> But all such babbling blockheads in his stead.
>   Let Sporus tremble. . . .[3]

> I lose my patience, and I own it too,
> When works are censur'd, not as bad but new;
> While if our Elders break all reason's laws,
> These fools demand not pardon, but Applause.
>   On Avon's bank, where flow'rs eternal blow
> If I but ask, if any weed can grow. . . .[4]

---

[1] *Mor. Ess.* iii. *Of the Use of Riches.* To Bathurst, 291 ff.
[2] *Epistle to Arbuthnot*, 145 ff.
[3] Id. 303 ff.
[4] *Im. of Hor.* Ep. ii. i. To Augustus, 115 ff.

> Yes, I am proud; I must be proud to see
> Men not afraid of God, afraid of me:
> Safe from the Bar, the Pulpit, and the Throne,
> Yet touch'd and sham'd by Ridicule alone.
>   O sacred weapon! left for Truth's defence. . . .[1]

Effects such as these show how much more subtle is the form of Pope's essays than that of Bacon's. The transitions provide some of his most intense moments.

Pope wrote some of his poems fast,[2] but corrected all his poems diligently. Usually his poems were composed piecemeal. But such poems did not satisfy him till, in the two years which usually intervened between composition and publication,[3] all traces of their desultory origins had been removed. The skill in dovetailing made it possible for him silently to add or subtract couplets and passages after a poem's first writing or publication. 'To make verses', said Dr. Johnson, 'was his first labour, and to mend them was his last.'[4] Professor Case's and Mr. Ault's discoveries of how much of his verse lies unacknowledged in the *Miscellany* of 1717 have recently provided further proof of Pope's standards before complete publication. Critics who hold that Pope left the traces of his piecemeal methods of composition, have failed to experience his work at its proper tempo. Poetry is generally much slower than prose and, among poems, those of Pope are particularly slow. They must be read slowly and often or their

---

[1] *Epilogue to Satires*, Dial. ii. 208 ff.   [2] See Spence, 142.
[3] *Lives*, ed. G. Birkbeck Hill, iii. 220.
[4] Id. 218. See Dodsley's evidence, id. 221.

finest qualities of meaning and workmanship will never be noticed at all. Given the proper attention, the snippets expand and cohere.

II

Three of Pope's mature poems required more than the horizontal continuity of an argument. *The Temple of Fame*, despite an incompletely stated connexion between the two temples, that of Fame and that of Rumour, is one of the most massively planned poetic *scenae* in English poetry. Then there are the *Rape of the Lock* and the *Dunciad* which are both based on the epic. The *Dunciad* follows *MacFlecknoe* in making the puppets of the satire go through a hollow, mean imitation of the heroic ritual of the epic. The more parallels to the epic, the more thorough is the incongruity. But the *Rape of the Lock* is the masterpiece in this manner because it provides a parallel to a complete epic poem. The *Dunciad*, like *MacFlecknoe*, is the ludicrous, grotesque, lifesize shadow cast by a piece of an epic poem, the *Rape of the Lock* an exquisitely diminished shadow cast by an entire epic, by the august epic form itself. Both these poems required not only a connected extension in time. They required also to be rounded into wholes. An epic poem, and so a mock epic poem, must seem to possess its own 'turning globe'. Aristotle's insistence on organic body-like structure was of vital importance here. The *Rape of the Lock* was perfectly rounded before the addition of the sylphs. This addition was worth risking almost at any cost. Spoiling the shape of the

4400

E

poem must almost have seemed unimportant after Pope had realized that this parody of the epic form contained no parody of its most obvious butt, the supernatural machinery. Pope's skill as an architect was never more exquisitely tested than when he attempted to transform the perfection of two cantos into that of five. The addition of the sylphs meant grafting wings on to a creature that had been planned for walking only. The task was almost impossible and Addison showed 'classic' wisdom in discountenancing a 'romantic' ambition. Addison was certainly justified before the event. And, despite Pope's instancing of the additions as the greatest proof of judgement he had ever shown,[1] Addison was probably also justified after the event. The second *Rape*, so much more brilliant than the first, is found by the nicest test not to be quite so correctly formed. The sylphs take up just a little too much space. But the operation of introducing them into the poem was performed with the perfect degree of subtlety. The sylphs are not planted over the poem in sealed hives. They are sometimes so planted, but at other times sent winging among the earlier elements of the poem. The best instance of this is at the actual moment of the rape. The first version (1712) reads:

> But when to Mischief Mortals bend their Mind,
> How soon fit Instruments of Ill they find?
> Just then, *Clarissa* drew with tempting Grace
> A two-edg'd Weapon from her shining Case;
> So Ladies in Romance assist their Knight,
> Present the Spear, and arm him for the Fight.

[1] Spence, 142.

He takes the Gift with rev'rence, and extends
The little Engine on his Finger[s'] Ends,
This just behind *Belinda*'s Neck he spread,
As o'er the fragrant Steams she bends her Head:
He first expands the glitt'ring *Forfex* wide
T'inclose the Lock; then joins it, to divide;
One fatal stroke the sacred Hair does sever
From the fair Head, for ever, and for ever!

I print the corresponding passage of 1714 from the edition of 1715, since that, apart from one small change, represents Pope's final text. (Two small errors of punctuation are corrected.)

But when to Mischief Mortals bend their Will,
How soon they find fit Instruments of Ill?
Just then, *Clarissa* drew with tempting Grace
A two-edg'd Weapon from her shining Case;
So Ladies in Romance assist their Knight,
Present their Spear, and arm him for the Fight.
He takes the Gift with Rev'rence, and extends
The little Engine on his Fingers Ends,
This just behind *Belinda*'s Neck he spread,
As o'er the fragrant Steams she bends her Head.
Swift to the Lock a thousand Sprights repair,
A thousand Wings by turns, blow back the Hair,
And thrice they twitch'd the Diamond in her Ear,
Thrice she look'd back, and thrice the Foe drew near.
Just in that instant, anxious *Ariel* sought
The close Recesses of the Virgin's Thought;
As on the Nosegay in her Breast reclin'd,
He watch'd th' Idea's rising in her Mind:
Sudden he view'd, in spite of all her Art,
An Earthly Lover lurking at her Heart.
Amaz'd, confus'd, he found his Power expir'd,
Resign'd to Fate, and with a Sigh retir'd.

The Peer now spreads the glitt'ring *Forfex* wide,
T''inclose the Lock; now joins it to divide.
Ev'n then, before the fatal Engine clos'd,
A wretched *Sylph* too fondly interpos'd;
Fate urg'd the Shears, and cut the *Sylph* in twain,
(But airy Substance soon unites again)
The meeting Points the sacred Hair dissever
From the fair Head, for ever and for ever!

Pope's task was almost impossible. The important thing is that he knew what exactly he wanted to do. He had the power of seeing a poem finished before it was begun, though in the *Rape of the Lock* there had to be two such visions. It is a rare compliment to an English poet that one can consider him seriously as a planner of large yet detailed designs.

A second attempt to alter a poem formerly left for finished is shown in the second main version of the *Dunciad*. Again, the first version in three Books is a better whole than the later in four. The fourth Book is an addition rather than a further growth. It shows the fulfilment of the prophecies in Book III and so is no more than a postscript. And in changing the hero from Theobald to Cibber Pope found old and superseded material too good to throw away. The relapse into yawns before the advent of the opiate goddess at the end of Book IV is less pleasing as narrative since it duplicates in idea the ending of Book II. And the famous conclusion, though cleverly sewn on, does not fit Book IV so well as it did Book III. And yet the misjointed construction that might wreck an epic does not wreck what is offered only as a piece of one, and especially when the verse is of the sort Pope provided here. The sense of the brilliant couplets is notoriously difficult to plumb, but the couplets when understood to a certain depth are found to be so compact, either individually or in groups, that the need for an onward sweep of heroic narrative is reduced to its minimum. Nor do we seek narrative from Book IV, which is a *scena* in the manner of *The Temple of Fame* rather than a length of story.

III

Pope paid unusual attention to the last paragraph of his poems. A favourite method was to close with an intense quiet reflective passage, uniting himself or more often the 'Muse' to the theme or person of his poem. *Windsor Forest* ends by Pope's seeking again 'the silent shade' of pastoral and leaving 'the thoughts of gods' to Granville's verse. In the *Essay on Criticism* Pope reflects on the passing of the master-and-pupil friendship between Walsh and himself. At the close of the *Rape of the Lock*, the Muse consecrates the Lock to fame. The *Temple of Fame* achieves a perfect close by taking, and making serious, a passage from the middle of the last book of Chaucer's unfinished poem, a passage in which Chaucer amusingly answers the question what he is doing trespassing in the House of Fame. Even *Eloisa to Abelard* and the *Elegy to the Memory of an Unfortunate Lady* end with personal codas. And the splendid speed of the fourth Epistle of the *Essay on Man* culminates in the soaring invocation to Bolingbroke:

Oh master of the poet and the song!

IV

Pope's concern for the whole may be measured by the growth of his dislike for description. He never wrote a poem which was all description, as, for example, Ambrose Philips did in his charming *Winter-Piece*.[1] But he began with a reverence for descriptive poetry and produced examples discreetly in some of his early poems. When making a small anthology of winter scenes for Caryll, he alludes to Homer, Virgil, Horace, and Milton as 'the greatest Genius's for Description'.[2] Chaucer is named to Spence as, among other things, 'a master of . . . description'.[3] As the human theme came to hold him more and more, Pope looked with intolerance on his early work in which, he vowed,

> . . . pure Description held the place of Sense.[4]

He slights the *Rape of the Lock* and *Windsor Forest* by hitting them off with the line

> A painted mistress, or a purling stream.[5]

This mature, purposely exaggerated verdict disregards the excellent quality of the descriptions in deprecating their quantity in length and number. There had been, for instance, the remarkable description of Zembla in the *Temple of Fame*:

> So Zembla's rocks (the beauteous work of frost)
> Rise white in air, and glitter o'er the coast;
> Pale suns, unfelt, at distance roll away,
> And on th'impassive ice the light'nings play;

[1] *Tatler*, No. 12.   [2] Letter of 21 Dec. 1712.
[3] p. 19.   [4] *Ep. to Arbuthnot*, 148.   [5] Id. 150.

Eternal snows the growing mass supply,
Till the bright mountains prop th'incumbent sky:
As Atlas fix'd, each hoary pile appears,
The gather'd winter of a thousand years.[1]

This made the mistake of describing too much, of trying to describe 'everything'.[2] When Zembla is mentioned in the *Dunciad*, it is significant that the mention is by name only:

Or gives to Zembla fruits, to Barca flow'rs.[3]

It is mentioned, and no more, in the *Essay on Man*.[4] If in these poems Pope had needed a description he would have limited himself to something like the second of those four couplets.

It is remarkable that even in the early work Pope's descriptions are never simply descriptions. They are always called for by the poem. They may, for instance, be bound to it by the ties of the simile. By the stricter tests of Pope's maturity, they outstay their welcome. Description in the later work, however, has always a whole batch of reasons requiring it; or an excuse is provided for it, as for instance in the original insertion in his imitation of Horace's sixth satire of Book II:

Behold the place, where if a Poet
Shin'd in Description, he might show it;
Tell how the Moon-beam trembling falls,
And tips with Silver all the walls;
Palladian walls, Venetian doors,
Grotesco roofs, and Stucco floors:

[1] 53 ff.   [2] Spence, 139–40.
[3] i. 74.   [4] ii. 224.

> But let it (in a word) be said,
> The Moon was up, and Men a bed,
> The Napkins white, the Carpet red. ⎵ 1

It is partly because of Pope's distrust of description that his poems lack those elements which his nineteenth-century critics thought him incapable of supplying.

---

1 187 ff. (the first part of the poem is Swift's work).

CORRECTNESS
III. LANGUAGE

I

THE poetic diction of good eighteenth-century poetry has been much misunderstood, and denunciation of it has sometimes been taken as automatic denunciation of the poetry as a whole. Pope's *Homer* was held responsible by Coleridge for most of this diction. And Coleridge did not stand alone in thinking it 'the main source of our pseudo-poetic diction'.[1] Southey held that it had 'done more than any, or all other books, towards the corruption of our poetry'.[2] Pope's *Homer* is certainly the greatest work in bulk and quality which used this diction. But Pope did not invent the diction. When he used it he was drawing from and adding to a fund which had been growing for more than a hundred years, a fund which had been augmented and improved by the 'progressive' poets of the seventeenth century, that is, by those who stand in the direct line of development.

II

The poetic diction of the eighteenth century may be said to begin, as far as English goes, in Sylvester's translation of Du Bartas, a poem in which ornamental extravagances are tumbled violently together. Sylvester's version of the *Divine Weeks* began to be

[1] *Biog. Lit.*, ed. Shawcross (1907), i. 26 n.
[2] *Correspondence*, ed. Dowden (1881), 224.

published in 1595 and, during the whole of the
seventeenth century, remained a dictionary of effects;
Drayton, William Browne, Sandys the translator of
Ovid, Benlowes, Milton, and Dryden are some of
the poets in its debt. Among the plethora of Sylvester's effects are several which, though not much
repeated by the Elizabethans, became increasingly
established in 'progressive' seventeenth-century and
eighteenth-century poetry. This in particular is what
happened to some of the methods of Sylvester's
brilliantly inventive language. Du Bartas and Sylvester were sometimes aiming at enriching their
effects by compression and they found that one way
of attaining this compression was by using verbs and
participial adjectives derived from Latin instead of
longer composite native equivalents. For example,
Sylvester writes:

> A novice Thief (that in a Closet spies
> A heap of Gold, that on the Table lies)
> Pale, fearfull shivering, twice or thrice extends,
> And twice or thrice retires his fingers' ends. . . .[1]

or

> Th'unpurged Aire to Water would resolve,
> And Water would the mountain tops involve.[2]

Eyes are spoken of as 'Heav'n-erected'.[3] A third
means of compression is that of phrases like 'an
yron River' and 'yron streamlings' (streams of
molten iron),[4] 'Iron Mistress' (of the loadstone),[5]

---

[1] II. i. 2 [i.e. *Second Part of the First Day of the II Weeke*] 338 ff. The
edition quoted from is Grosart's in the *Chertsey Worthies' Library* (1878).
[2] I. iv. 590-1.   [3] II. i. 4. 428.
[4] Id. 493 and 515.   [5] I. iii. 952.

'watery Camp' (compare Virgil's *campi liquentes*, for the sea),[1] 'Heav'nly Round' (the sky),[2] 'she *Fills* her forkèd Round' (of the moon),[3] 'Scaly crew' (fishes),[4] and so on. These are pictorial methods of compression which Du Bartas found in Latin poetry. Virgil has phrases like *ferreus imber* (shower of weapons) and *ferrea . . . telorum seges* (an iron harvest of spears).[5] In his version of the Atalanta story, Ovid not only refers to one of the apples as 'nitidique pomi' but as 'aurumque volubile'.[6] Sandys (1626) translates the latter phrase as 'rowling gold'. Virgil in the *Culex* writes

apricas
pastor agit curas,[7]

'sunny cares' meaning the shepherd's piping. Lucan, speaking of bees, has the phrase 'laboris floriferi'[8] which Thomas May (1627) translates as 'flow'ry taskes'. Sandys liked these effects enough to multiply them beyond Ovid's number. Sylvester had liked the formula [epithet] + 'round', and Chapman had imitated him in the line

> While th'Ocean walks in storms his wavy round.[9]

And so Sandys when he comes on Ovid's

> . . . qua totum Nereus circumsonat orbem[10]

translates it by

> Wher-euer Nereus walks his wauy round.

---

[1] Id. 993.   [2] I. iv. 217.   [3] Id. 476.
[4] I. v. 33.   [5] *Aeneid*, xii. 284, and iii. 45–6.
[6] *Met.* x. 666–7.
[7] 98–9.   [8] *Civil War*, ix. 289–90.
[9] *Byron's Tragedy*, iv. 1.   [10] *Met.* i. 187.

Again, Sandys invents the phrase 'wavy monarchy' where there is nothing in the Latin to require it.[1]

These are effects which grow in popularity. Sylvester has his iron mistress, and iron river, Pope his 'iron squadrons' (battleships),[2] his 'iron harvests of the field',[3] his 'leaden death',[4] his 'scaly breed'.[5]

One cannot go farther and claim for Sylvester any extensive influence on the specific vocabulary of this later poetry. He does have a predilection for certain words (*alternate*, *trembling*, for instance) which become prominent in later poetic diction, but their force is almost lost in the general heterogeneity of his vocabulary. (It is the same with Shakespeare,

> that ocean where each kind
> Does straight its own resemblance find;

many of these words occur in the plays but are not salient). It was probably not Sylvester, but his imitator Sandys, who did most to fix the vocabulary of 'progressive' English poetry for more than a century. These increasingly favourite words of Sandys may be seen forming themselves into a group all the more clearly because his vocabulary is much more selective than Sylvester's. Sandys has not the unlimited space that Sylvester chose to tumble about in. His aim in translating Ovid was to produce a version in the same number of lines as the original. In this severe task he was almost literally successful, and that despite the shackles of rime, a pentameter line instead of an hexameter, and the English lan-

[1] *Met.* ii. circa 290.
[2] *Windsor Forest*, 363.
[3] *Essay on Man*, iv. 12.
[4] *Windsor Forest*, 132.
[5] Id. 139.

guage instead of the Latin. To attain his end, he had
to stiffen up the natural laxity of English (*a*) by
latinizing his syntax (though he does not offend in
this by excess), (*b*) by imitating the Latin use of
present and past participles as adjectives, (*c*) by using
verbs derived from Latin instead of composite
English verbs. But equally important for later
poetry is Sandys's group of favourite and semi-
favourite words: *anxious* (often with `cares`), *pensive*,
*ratify, promiscuous(ly), sad, trembling, glittering, nodding,
sylvan, refulgent, pale, alternate, sing* (of hail and
arrows), *yielding, involve*. Among these an important
word is *sad*. Sandys's liking for this word may be
due to the place the pathetic came to hold in Silver
Latin poetry, a province of Latin poetry which came
more and more into esteem. As Latin poetry grew
more fierce and heroic with Statius and Lucan, it
grew also more melancholy. Pathos drips thick as
blood when events require. Sandys, for whatever
cause, is charmed by the word. Ovid's account of
the fate of Orpheus contains the following lines:

> Te maestae volucres, Orpheu, te turba ferarum,
> te rigidi silices, te carmina saepe secutae
> fleverunt silvae, positis te frondibus arbor
> tonsa comas luxit; lacrimis quoque flumina dicunt
> increvisse suis, obstrusaque carbasa pullo
> naides et dryades passosque habuere capillos.
> membra iacent diversa locis, caput, Hebre, lyramque
> excipis: et (mirum!) medio dum labitur amne,
> flebile nescio quid queritur lyra, flebile lingua
> murmurat exanimis, respondent flebile ripae.[1]

[1] *Met.* xi. 44–53.

Sandys's translation makes Ovid resemble a Silver
Latin poet by using *sad* five times:

Sad birds, wilde Heards, hard flints, and woods, of late
Led by thy verse, then wept: at thy sad fate
Trees shed their leaues: streames with their teares increast:
The *Naiades* and *Dryades* inuest
Themselues in sullen sable, and display
Their scattered haire. Thy limbes dispersed lay.
His head and harp they into *Hebrus* flung,
The harp sounds something, sadly; the dead tongue
Sighes out sad ditties: the bankes sympathize
(That bound the riuer) in their sad replies.

In Golding's translation of these lines, done some sixty
years earlier, *sad* is not used once. Sandys's partiality for
the word is not simply due to its being a monosyllable,
and so leaving his heavily chartered line with nine
syllables to spare. He likes the word for its own sake.

But it is Thomas May in his translation of Lucan
(1626–27) who opens the flood gates. Lucan is an
author with much more liking for the pathetic than
had even the author of the *Tristia*, but May exagger-
ates even the amount that Lucan provides. Whatever
form the pathetic word takes in Lucan, May will
translate it by *sad*: *tristis* (e.g. v. 32, 57, 753), *maestus*
(e.g. v. 15, 391, 442, 741, 761, 774, 792, 797),
maerere (e.g. v. 115), *funestus* (e.g. vi. 6, vii. 167),
luctificus (vii. 2), *miser* (vii. 416), *miserabilis* (ix. 832).
On scores of occasions it is introduced by May
without warrant from Lucan. Indeed the word
dazzles him to the point of making him translate
saeva fames[1] not as 'fierce' but as 'sad famine': the

[1] iv. 94.

same thing happens to *saeva* again at viii. 704: *bubone sinistro*[1] (with an owl on the left) becomes 'sad owles'; *dira* becomes 'sad' at iv. 790; at viii. 589 *sad* is introduced although it spoils the sense. Something like the same honour is paid to *trembling* (adjective) and (in much smaller degree) to *tremble*. It is a favourite word of Sylvester and Sandys but, again, with May partiality has become passion. In using *trembling* he receives more encouragement from his original, but perpetually improves on it: *trembling* (with occasionally *tremble*) is given as the equivalent, for example, of Lucan's *trementi* (v. 152), *tremuit* (v. 364), *trepidam* (v. 381), *fragilem* (v. 595: with *malum* 'mainemast', though *volitantia* is not translated), *trepidant* (vi. 417), *timentem* (vi. 721), *tremulo* (vi. 87), *horruit* (viii. 342). *Trembling* is also used without warrant from Lucan at iii. 731–2.

May similarly overtops Lucan in his fondness for *soft*. For example in his translation of ix. 49–50 his *soft* has literally no more warrant than his *sad*:

> But those sad ships brought griefe, and woes, and cryes
> Able to draw soft teares from *Cato*'s eyes.[2]

In Rowe's translation of Lucan (1718) the process is seen still augmenting itself. If the incident of Cornelia's grief at Pompey's grave is compared in both versions, May's is found to have one unwarranted *sad*, Rowe's four.[3] Rowe also continues the process begun by May of exaggerating the 'softness' of Lucan. Ogilby's translations of the *Æneid* (1649),

[1] v. 396.   [2] Ed. 1635, sig. P 6r.
[3] In the corresponding passage in Sir Arthur Gorges's translation of Lucan into tetrameter couplets (1614) none of these words are used.

the *Iliad* (1660), and the *Odyssey* (1665) make fair
use of these words. Ogilby's *Homer* and Sandys's *Ovid*
were the first long poems which Pope read:

Ogilby's translation of Homer was one of the first large
poems that ever Mr. Pope read; and he still spoke of the
pleasure it then gave him, with a sort of rapture, only in
reflecting on it.—'It was the great edition with pictures,'
I was then about eight years old. This led me to Sandys's
Ovid, which I liked extremely . . .'[1]

Pope came to think Ogilby's poetry 'too mean for
criticism'[2] just as Dryden came to think his early idol,
Sylvester, 'abominable fustian'.[3] But their 'pleasure'
and 'ecstasy' over these idealized poets in childhood
meant more for their own poetry than any adult
recantation could undo.

Most of the seventeenth-century poets who are
not metaphysicals or satirists build up their vocabulary from Sandys and from Sandys's sources.
Milton's minor poems and, to a less extent, his
major poems, show the debt to Sylvester and Sandys
perfectly combined among all those other debts to
earlier English poetry. Milton uses *sad*, for example,
fifty-one times and the allied words *sadness*, *saddest*,
and *sadly* seven times. The most memorable uses of
sad are found in the minor poems:

Bitter constraint, and sad occasion dear (*Lycidas*, 6).
And every flower that sad embroidery wears (id. 148).
Like a sad Votarist in Palmer's weed (*Comus*, 189).
Nightly to thee her sad Song mourneth well (id. 235).

The minor poems, too, show consummate use of

[1] Spence, 276.   [2] *Iliad*, Preface, folio edition, I [*first series*] 2ᵛ.
[3] See p. 78 below.

pensive, trembling, &c. Milton's use of these words, along with Waller's, seals their aristocracy. Both poets contribute new words of their own to the growing fund.

All these words come thickly in Dryden, especially in his non-satiric poems—in his rimed heroic dramas and 'translations'. They come plentifully in certain poems and parts of poems of Pope. In the *Rape of the Lock*, *trembling* and *tremble(s)* come eight times, *soft* four times, *soften('d)* twice, *softer* twice, *glitt'ring* five times, *sad* three times, *anxious* twice, *bright(est)* (a favourite word of Milton) five times. (Other favourite words are *beauteous, shining, melting, glowing*.[1] The former two, at least, are common in later seventeenth-century poetry.) *Eloisa to Abelard*, a poem of 366 lines, repeats *sad* twelve times, *sadness, sadly*, and *saddens* once each. *Trembling* and *tremble(d)* come seven times, and *soft* four times (and the allied words *tears, sighs* and *weep* very frequently since the theme is what it is). The quality of Pope's general meaning and the quality of the versification renews the poignancy in these worn words. But it must not be overlooked that the main impression of *Eloisa* is one of almost luxurious pleasure.

III

The diction of the seventeenth- and eighteenth-century poets has been attacked by later critics

---

[1] The history of *shining* is worth a note. William Barrett, the Bristol antiquary whom Chatterton duped, repeatedly told Jacob Bryant that Chatterton's gifts were 'by no means shining'. This degraded, almost slangy use in prose persists in our 'shining example'.

principally on three grounds: (*a*) that it was a new borrowing from Latin, for example *dehorting*, or that it used in their original Latin sense words which were already borrowed and developed in meaning, for example *obvious*; (*b*) that it adapted a Latin method of phrasing, for example, *fleecy care*; and (*c*) that it was used too much.

There is no appeal against the excessive use of this diction except that only bad poets use it to excess. Against objection (*a*), there are two replies possible. In the first place these poets were experimenters. The future history of language could alone show that they were innovating their Latinisms too freely. At the time of the innovation there was no telling which words would and which words would not lose their virtue. The unknown factor was

> . . . Time (whose slippery wheel doth play
> In humane causes with inconstant sway,
> Who exiles, alters, and disguises words.)[1]

Sylvester and Sandys stood in the middle and at the close of the 'Elizabethan' period, a period when invention in language was universally practised. Sylvester and Sandys were among these coiners of words, as Milton was later. Many of their words died, except perhaps for their history in poetry. But this is what happened to many of Milton's, too.

But the linguistic practice of Sylvester and Sandys included also another device. They saw the possibility of enriching English by using, in their literal Latin sense, words which were derived from Latin

---

[1] Sylvester's *Divine Weeks*, II. i. 1. 204 ff.

in the first place but which had developed a different meaning in English. This was no merely academic aim since the contemporary knowledge of Latin was general among readers of poetry. And there is no doubt that this device, when it is understood, provides pleasure. When the reader has discovered that the word is bearing a literal meaning, he is aware of an increase in neatness, since the English way of arriving at the same meaning is often longer in the number of its words. The accurate estimating of this kind of effect is now impossible since one can never be certain how far these words had developed from their original Latin meaning and how far that meaning had been overlaid. The *O.E.D.* provides help. For example, it records concerning *obvious* that Drayton used it in the literal sense of 'fronting' in 1603, that this sense is found in poetry as late as 1814, that Quarles uses it, in 1635, in its developed English sense of 'manifest, palpable'. Here the word seems to have retained its literal sense along with its developed one. But the new sense is found frequently enough to have probably given the literal *obvious* of Milton, John Philips, Pope, and Akenside an effect of conscious purity. (Each word in the poetic diction must be examined separately, and it must be remembered that the exact linguistic effects of two or three hundred years ago are now impossible to synthesize.)

The justification of a phrase like 'fleecy care' is much more complex. In the first place there was the contemporary justification that it was Latin and therefore in itself providing cultivated pleasure. Our

own age requires more than that, as the good poets
of the seventeenth and eighteenth centuries required
more than that. *Fleecy care* is good as sound. It is
also subtle and complex as meaning. The meanings
of *cura* as given in Lewis and Short's dictionary are:
care, solicitude, thought, attention, management,
command, guardianship, healing, culture, rearing,
anxiety, the cares of love, the beloved. Most of these
are possible meanings for *care* in English, and all of
them are applicable to the relationship between
shepherd and sheep. A complex relationship stands
in that phrase almost completely stated. It is much
more subtle as a phrase than Shakespeare's 'woolly
breeders' in the *Merchant of Venice*.[1] Of course it
served as model for less good phrases: 'vegetable
care', for example, although a dignified expression at
that time, cannot equally bear all the connotations of
cura, since plants are virtually inanimate.

Considered more generally this kind of phrase provides an excellent method of compression, especially
since it is often an abstract and a concrete which are
clashed together. Such combinations surprise the
reader—on the face of it the two elements are so
unlikely as concomitants. The combining of them
in the intimate relationship of noun and epithet
requires from him a special process of apprehension.
The reader has first to analyse the phrase into its
separate parts and then to draw them together again
in what has become for him a richer, because fully
comprehended, unity. This method of compression
by periphrasis, of comprehensive description and

[1] I. iii. 84.

designation acting simultaneously, becomes one of the most prominent items in the poetic diction of the eighteenth century.

Another favourite phrase is [*adjective*] + a group word: for example, *the feather'd kind*. When Sylvester used 'Scaly crew' he was frankly engaged in decorating his verse, a quite laudable objective. He was not engaged in avoiding the word *fish*—Sylvester was afraid of no word, native or foreign, invented or inventable. But later poets often write *scaly kind* because they fear to spoil the prettiness of their poem with *fish*. They feel acutely the dilemma of Virgil in the *Georgics*. Virgil had been troubled by the unpoetic frankness of his material. His problem as Dryden translated it, ran:

> Nor can I doubt what Oyl I must bestow,
> To raise my Subject from a Ground so low:
> And the mean Matter which my Theme affords,
> T'embellish with Magnificence of Words.[1]

The poetic conscience behind that weighed heavily with poets who regarded Virgil with awe. Virgil had got over his difficulty partly by ignoring it and writing straight ahead of scabs and foot-rot, and partly by relying on phrases consecrated to the epic and on the spell of his versification. The poets of the georgic poetry of the eighteenth century and of the allied local poetry which began with *Cooper's Hill*, aim at a stateliness befitting Virgil's conception of poetry. The poets of the eighteenth century attain gracefulness, as Virgil did, by their metre. And more than Virgil needed to do, they attain it by avoiding

[1] iii. 453 ff.

low words like *fish* and *sheep*. But in the work of
good poets the periphrases are not there simply or
primarily because they avoid a low word, nor even
because they provide decoration—'fleecy care', for
instance, may make a beautiful contribution to the
sound of a passage. In the work of good poets they
are there often because they help the precision of
the meaning. Milton spoke of a moonlit 'finny
drove'[1] because, first of all, he wanted the reader to
be aware of an exquisite battery of fins. And in
Windsor Forest and *The Seasons*, similar phrases are
used when the meaning calls for them. This is not
as often as the meaning *fish* (plural) and *birds* arises,
but only when fish and birds are being thought of as
distinct in their appearance or material entity from
other groups of creatures. Both Pope and Thomson
use *fish* and *birds* whenever they want to. And they
specify in uncompromisingly straightforward terms
what particular fish or bird they mean when they
mean it—carp, pike, pheasant, lapwing, woodcock.
But when they are thinking of fish as fish are distinct
from birds or beasts, they employ the formula which
embodies the distinction. When Thomson speaks of
the sportsmen with 'gun' and 'spaniel' who

> Distress the Feathery, or the Footed *Game*[2]

he is not merely decorating his poem, but differen-
tiating the game that is hit while it flies from the
game that is hit while it runs. When Thomson calls
birds 'the glossy kind' it is because he is going on to

---

[1] *Comus*, 115.
[2] *Winter* (1st edition), 324.

show how that glossiness counts in the mating season, when the male birds

> . . . shiver every feather with desire.[1]

When Thomson speaks of young birds as 'the feather'd youth' he means that the birds, though young, are not too young to have feathers, and that they resemble young human beings decked in new finery. Pope uses 'scaly breed' for fish because he has been speaking of game birds, and particularly of the partridge with its 'shining plumes' and 'breast that flames with gold', and is now changing to another kind of game, one with a different covering (scales instead of feathers) but one, otherwise, splendidly the same:

> The silver eel, in *shining* volumes roll'd,
> The yellow carp, in *scales* bedropp'd with *gold*.[2]

There is also another reason for this poetic diction. It is notable that it is principally used in reference to external nature. The eighteenth century inherited the Renaissance creed that man is monarch in his world. And although Dryden and Pope often look on external nature, as Thomson did, for what it could show them of splendour or beauty or even of mystery, they are often engaged in allotting it a due and fit place in the human scheme. They were often concerned with seeing external nature not as they knew it deserved to be seen but as they wanted to see it. They superimposed on nature what they considered at certain times to be desirable. They made a selection from nature of elements that suited

---

[1] *Spring*, 630.   [2] *Windsor Forest*, 117 ff.

their interests. This is what all poets do. Dryden, Pope, and the rest differ from many poets only in what they superimpose and in what they select. They superimposed on nature some of their own civilized humanity. Shakespeare had superimposed human qualities on nature. He saw waves, for instance, as striving, as if they were beasts or men (or, more truly, perhaps as if they were boys). Romeo sees the severing clouds as envious. Sylvester outdid all the Elizabethans by superimposing the most sophisticated humanity he could find. Dryden admits that

when I was a boy, I thought inimitable Spenser a mean poet, in comparison of Sylvester's *Dubartas*, and was rapt into an ecstasy when I read these lines:

> *Now, when the Winter's keener breath began*
> *To chrystallize the Baltick Ocean;*
> *To glaze the Lakes, to bridle up the Floods,*
> *And periwig with Snow the bald-pate Woods.*

His comment on this boyish enthusiasm is severe now that he is fifty:

I am much deceived if this be not abominable fustian, that is, thoughts and words ill-sorted, and without the least relation to each other.[1]

But Dryden himself was often doing in his own way what Sylvester had done in his more headlong way. Later poets also develop Sylvester's system. Pope, who had a fair esteem for Sylvester,[2] is found once at least superimposing the same sophisticated human item. The occasion

Of the going backe of the Sun in the time of Ezekias

---

[1] *Dedication of the Spanish Friar*, 1681. Ker's ed. i. 247.
[2] See Spence, 22.

provides Sylvester with the kind of opportunity which excited his fancy:

> Thy Coach turn'd back, and thy swift sweating Horse
> Full ten degrees lengthned their wonted Course:
> *Dials* went false, and Forrests (gloomy black)
> Wondred to see their mighty shades go back.[1]

Pope has his forests acting in an identically human way:

> O'er sandy wilds were yellow harvests spread,
> The forests wonder'd at th'unusual grain.[2]

Their regard for man made them a little haughty among stars, trees, and animals. For the Augustans

> . . . man superior walks
> Amid the glad creation

—the words surprisingly are Thomson's.[3] In their belief that nature is controlled by man the Augustans resembled their hero Virgil, whose *Georgics* rejected the belief of Lucretius that the productiveness of nature was on the wane for the belief that 'the earth if rightly dealt with' would never refuse 'the "imperium" of man'.[4] Charles II's rigidly controlled garden at St. James's with its Mall, its rectangular sheets of water (the 'canal'), its borders of equispaced limes, showed that man's control of nature could be virtually complete within limits, just as for Virgil it could be as complete as Rome's control over a conquered people. They controlled nature perfectly in their gardens. But the landscape proved less tractable, though the Kents and Capability Browns did

---

[1] I. iv. 836 ff. [2] *Windsor Forest*, 88–9.
[3] *Spring*, 170–1.
[4] The words are Cicero's, quoted by W. Y. Sellar, *The Roman Poets of the Augustan Age*, Virgil (1877), 208.

their best. Mental control over landscape, however, could be complete at will, as Ovid had shown. And this is what happens in their pastorals and allied poetry by a kind of wish-fulfilment.

The theme of the pastoral was one of man, but it was man at his faintest. An age which valued satire could only amuse itself in pastoral. Man is the theme still, but it is man as a pretty creature, provided with set and toy emotions which last only to the end of the poem. The melodious tear was shed, the lips were silked with a smile, and all this was done out of doors. The traditions of pastoral forbade this out-of-doors to be a garden. It had to be landscape. But the landscape, in verse at least, could be perfectly made to own man's imperium.

The pastoralists therefore controlled its appearance in their verse with the same rigid hand that King Charles's gardeners had used on the configuration of St. James's Park. They 'methodized' it by taming it in diction, by caging it in a small group of words which satisfied their garden-bred sense of elegance. This sense of elegance required simplification. The landscape, always limited in pastoral, was further limited by being robbed of all characteristics except those which proved its gentleness, its tamedness. The brook could be there but should be a stream. It should purl rather than babble. The qualities of the word *stream* cleared away all the pebbles and angles of the brook, canalized it. If the noise of the stream, its purl, was for some reason undesirable in a line, its purity would be chemically certified as *crystal*. There should be meadows or meads. There

should be woods, but not so near that you could see
any 'knotty, knarry barren treës old'. The woods
should be beheld distantly and seen as a whole, and
seen as *waving*. This is how they composed their
'sylvan scenes', a phrase which they borrow from
Milton. The imperium of man was further insisted
on by the frequent allusion to nature in terms of
what man adapted from it for his own use: lawns
were *velvet*, sheep *fleecy*. Nature was shown as
imitating art—even the fields of heaven for Isaac
Watts 'stand *drest* in living green'. The landscapes
of Broome and Fenton, both published in the
'Miscellany' of 1712, show with what uniform completeness external nature could be commanded.
Broome writes:

> Thee, Shepherd, thee the pleasurable Woods,
> The painted Meadows, and the Crystal Floods,
> Claim, and invite thee to their sweet Abodes.[1]

And a little later he goes on with 'There Fountains
warble. . . .' Fenton, some thirty pages farther on,
has the line

> Ye warbling Fountains, and ye Chrystal Floods.[2]

The motto of both these passages is *Everything
of the Best*. Broome and Fenton are self-elected
Tweedledum and Tweedledee. They are two poets
playing for safety. But among the better pastoral
poets, though the material is virtually the same, the
sense of the ready-made is defeated. The pastorals
of Pope, of Ambrose Philips, and of Gay (when he

---

[1] *The Complaint. Cælia to Damon.*
[2] *Rapin Imitated, in a Pastoral . . .*

outgrows his wish to parody) employ the recognized diction, but their styles are as distinct as the different flavours of cheese. To amplify one instance: Mr. C. V. Deane, in an admirably thoughtful study, shows how Pope's manuscript of the *Pastorals* exhibits the contemporary diction seeking and attaining exactitude of music and statement. 'It cannot be said . . . that in the *Pastorals* Pope's poetic diction becomes a substitute for poetic feeling.'[1] The eighteenth century liked a restriction which operated before the poem was begun, which operated as a condition of the 'inspiration'. Inside that restriction they could keep holiday and the best of them did. And they took advantage of a law which operates in poetry as in everything else, the law of scale, of proportion. They knew that a reader soon scrambles on to the level of the poem and that, when he has reached it, that level becomes his norm. In *Endymion* everything is so exotic that, to provide a surprise, Keats almost has to burst a blood-vessel. In Gray's *Elegy* the even tenor of the style gives a word like *tinklings* the equivalence of an 'angelic strength', and this, despite the common occurrence of the word in the poetry of his immediate predecessors. Fenton, small poet as he is, counts on the benefits of this law. A few lines after the line quoted above, he introduces the phrase 'living Fountains' and with all the more effectiveness after his poetic sleep. Bolder and better poets used this law to the full, especially after the heartening example of Dryden, whose verbs are more energetic than those of any other English poet.

[1] *Aspects of Eighteenth Century Nature Poetry* (1935), 116.

The modern reader can find in this 'nature methodised'[1] a legitimate pleasure. It is a milder pleasure than that afforded by contemplation of the Ptolemaic idea of the universe, or the eternal idea of the stars with their mathematical accuracy and yet each star a flaming mass. But at bottom it is the same pleasure. The storm in Ovid's story of Ceyx and Alcyone and Dryden's translation of it are examples of tumult fettered accurately in verse to the point of forcing some readers to exclaim with pleasure. And since Pope and his contemporaries held Deistic opinions, the contemplation afforded still further pleasure. But for all that, these poets knew that the pastoral was a deception. Dryden knew that even the pastorals of Virgil were play-things, and vented the denied interests of his mind by translating

> est mihi namque domi pater, est iniusta noverca[2]

by

> A Stepdame too I have, a cursed she,
> Who rules my Hen-peck'd Sire, and orders me.

The gusto even of human triviality was powerful enough to break into Dryden's pastoral, even into man's chosen holiday from life. And the force of the tempest was more powerful still. For all man's fore-thought, for all his art, there might fall a 'universal darkness', ruining more than his shielded pastoral. Pope's

> The fox obscene to gaping tombs retires,
> And savage howlings fill the sacred quires,[3]

---

[1] *Ess. on Crit.* 89. I am, of course, giving the phrase a connotation Pope did not intend.   [2] *Ecl.* iii. 33.   [3] *Windsor Forest*, 71–2.

and Dyer's adaptation

> 'Tis now the raven's bleak abode;
> 'Tis now th' apartment of the toad;
> And there the fox securely feeds . . .[1]

and Gray's more powerful adaptation

> Purg'd by the sword and beautifyed by fire,
>   Then had we seen proud London's hated walls,
> Owls might have hooted in St. Peters Quire,
>   And foxes stunk and litter'd in St. Pauls.[2]

Or there is Thomas Warton the elder's

> O'er venerable Virgins sculptur'd Heads,
> Nods horrid Thorn, and darksome Elder spreads,
> And with close Foliage o'er the pictur'd Walls,
> Time's favourite Plant the mournful Ivy crawls . . .[3]

And, later, Cunningham's

> The lizard and the lazy lurking bat
>   Inhabit now, perhaps, the painted room. . . .[4]

In passages such as these, in Dryden's and Thomson's storms, in Gray's dread and courage among mountains, the 'age of reason' acknowledged the enormous forces of man's environment.

IV

Pope believes that there is a correctness of diction. Certain poems require to draw from a fund of acknowledged poetic diction, others require original diction. In discussing the problem of diction in the *Essay on Criticism*,[5] Pope makes no reference to

[1] *Grongar Hill*, 77 ff.
[2] *Verses on Lord Holland's Villa*, 21 ff.
[3] *Verses on Henry the Eighth's seizing the Abbey Lands, and on Queen Anne's Augmentation of Livings*, 37 ff.
[4] *Elegy on a Pile of Ruins*, 77–8.   [5] 305 ff.

poetic diction. He requires that language should be appropriate.[1] There should be no incongruity between the length in space (or time) and the length in meaning, between decoration and substance, between obsolete and modern. The poet should use words which will not arouse the discomfort of a correct person by being too archaic or too slangy. The *Peri Bathous*, later, was to arraign those imitators of Milton whose imitation extended no further than writing *nathless* instead of *nevertheless*, *eremites* instead of *hermits*, &c.[2] The poet is almost as free when writing poetry as he is when writing prose or conversing in public. The ideal of appropriateness denies the right of domination to any prescribed anthology of correct words. His practice, however, shows that he realized that the 'poetic diction' could at times be itself appropriate. He always used language, as Horace had counselled, according to plan.[3] He informed Spence that if he were correcting the language of an elegy, for example, he might say 'these lines are very good, but are they not of too heroical a strain?'[4] Pope follows many critics before him in requiring first of all that language should be appropriate. Appropriateness was a cardinal virtue for Pope in life as well as literature. In a letter of the 19 November 1712, he told Caryll that he wished to be a wit only on appropriate occasions:

... I have known an author, who for having once written a tragedy has never been out of buskins since: he can no more

[1] The importance of 'propriety' had been excellently stated in Dryden's Preface to *Albion and Albanius* (1685).

[2] Chap. ix.   [3] *Ars Poetica*, 86–98.   [4] p. 23.

suffer a vulgar phrase in his own mouth than in a Roman's . . .
For my part there are some things I would be thought besides
a wit,—as a christian, a friend, a frank companion, and a
well-natured fellow. . . . .

In the words of the *Essay on Criticism*:

> Expression is the dress of thought, and still
> Appears more decent, as more suitable. . . .
> For diff'rent styles with diff'rent subjects sort,
> As several garbs with country, town, and court.[1]

Even letters must be written appropriately and what
is appropriate to one distinguished from what is
appropriate to another.

It is idle to say that letters should be written in an easy
familiar style: that, like most other general rules, will not
hold. The style, in letters as in all other things, should be
adapted to the subject.[2]

Addison failed to adapt himself to this rule:

Mr. Addison could not give out a common order in writing,
from his endeavouring always to word it too finely. He had
too beautiful an imagination to make a man of business.[3]

Pope even has a rule for the appropriate placing of
prepositions:

'What is your opinion [asks the Boswellian Spence] of
placing prepositions at the end of a sentence?'—It is certainly
wrong: but I have made a rule to myself about them some
time ago, and I think verily 'tis the right one. We use them
so in common conversation: and that use will authorize one,
I think, for doing the same in slighter pieces, but not in
formal ones. In a familiar letter for instance, but not in a

---

[1] 318 ff.   [2] Spence, 176.   [3] Id. 175.

weighty one: and more particularly in dialogue writing, but then it must be when the people introduced are talking, and not where the author appears in his own person.[1]

Pope's own regard for appropriateness can be seen at its smallest in his distinction between 'em and them, a distinction which some of his editors have not understood.

Pope cannot endure stiffness. He told Spence that Parnell's essay on Homer affixed to the *Iliad*

is still stiff; and was written much stiffer. As it is, I think verily it cost me more pains in the correcting, than the writing of it would have done.[2]

Shakespeare is arraigned because 'for the speeches of his kings and great men' he 'generally used to stiffen his style with high words and metaphors'.[3] Another opinion expressed to Spence was that

I have nothing to say for rhyme, but that I doubt whether a poem can support itself without it, in our language; unless it be stiffened with such strange words, as are likely to destroy our language itself.[4]

Blackmore exemplified the defect:

A Voice there is, that whispers in my ear,
('Tis Reason's voice, which sometimes one can hear)
'Friend Pope! be prudent, let your Muse take breath,
And never gallop Pegasus to death;
Lest stiff, and stately, void of fire or force,
You limp, like Blackmore on a Lord Mayor's horse.'[5]

The verb *stiffen* had been used before in reflections on Blackmore in the *Peri Bathous*.[6] The stiff poet

---

[1] Id. 213.   [2] p. 138.   [3] p. 173.   [4] p. 200.
[5] *Im. of Hor.* Ep. I. i. To Bolingbroke. 11 ff.   [6] Chap. vi.

was one who had a defective sense of what was verbally appropriate.

V

How does this principle of appropriate diction and style apply to the poems? The 'poetic' diction of the *Pastorals* is appropriate because Pope is writing imitations. His subject is not shepherds, but shepherds as they appear in classical pastorals. The diction of *Windsor Forest* is appropriate for similar reasons. Pope's inspiration for the poem is not 'Georgian'—that is, it does not derive simply from a familiar expanse of woodland. The vision of trees was from the first complicated, civilized, by the historical and political connotations of the place. And still more, it was complicated by the work of earlier poets—of Denham and, what is more important, of Virgil and Ovid. (Pope's inspiration is always partly a literary one.) His language must therefore have an intellectual dignity if it is to be appropriate for the more than topographical complexity of the subject-matter. Wordsworth's *Yew Trees* has its dignified language. Yew trees are themselves dignified and, further, they lead Wordsworth to think of Umfraville and Percy, of Agincourt, Crecy, and Poictiers. But the dignity of Wordsworth's poem is not further intellectualized by any literary reverence for another age of poetry. Before Pope came to write a line of *Windsor Forest*, he had invested the place with the presence of Virgil and his *Georgics*, of Ovid and his *Metamorphoses*. The finished poem, therefore, bears the combined influence of the glades, fables, and hexameters. His language is appropriate, though not simple. It is as simple as it can be without being inappropriate.

There is no 'diction' in the satires, though there are touches in the *Dunciad* necessary for conveying the mock heroics. Ruffhead in his *Life of Pope* blames Pope for using the low words *cups* and *spoons* in the *Rape of the Lock*:

There is great merit likewise in painting the scene of the tea-table . . . though the same dignity and elegance is not preserved as in the [description of the game of ombre]. The introductory line is particularly faulty. . . . The appellations of *Cups* and *Spoons* in this place, are too low and common; and they ought to have been mentioned with a periphrasis to have preserved the mock dignity of the piece. Mr Pope was here unmindful of Horace's remark——

'*Difficile est propriè communia dicere.*'[1]

Pope does periphrase cups five lines later as 'China's earth', but this is mainly because he is avoiding, like most English writers, the too close repetition of a word. Pompous periphrasis is one of many butts in the *Peri Bathous*. Instead of *shut the door* (an expression which Pope was to use as the opening of the *Epistle to Arbuthnot*) the foolish write

> The wooden guardian of our privacy
> Quick on its axle turn.[2]

In the moral poetry Pope uses words almost with the freedom and fearlessness of Shakespeare.

This freedom can be seen nowhere more readily than in Pope's verbs, especially when it is remembered that the verbs of the 'poetic diction' were

[1] *Life of Alexander Pope* (1769), 117.   [2] Chap. xii.

predominantly of Latin origin. Here are some of
them:

> There Affectation . . .
> Faints into airs . . .[1]
>
> Old Politicians chew on wisdom past[2]
>
> . . . before a sprightlier age
> Comes titt'ring on, and shoves you from the stage.[3]
>
> When Int'rest calls off all her sneaking train[4]
>
> No creature smarts so little as a fool.[5]

Pope is free. But even here he is not free to use
any word that comes into his head, since, like all his
poems, the satires are addressed to the cultured society of the time. Poeticisms are barred. There must
be no merely ornamental epithets, and no compound
ones. The epithet must therefore fall into its prose
order, that is, it must precede the noun (it was
partly the inversion of prose order which irritated
Dr. Johnson in the poems of Collins and Thomas
Warton).[6] Pope makes very few exceptions to these

---

[1] *Rape of the Lock*, iv, 31 ff. According to *O.E.D.*, Pope coined this
composite verb, and Keats was the only other writer to use it. Pope
has several daring coinages of this kind; for example:

> . . . The proud Parnassian sneer,
> The conscious simper, and the jealous leer,
> Mix on his look . . .

(*Dunc.* ii. 5 ff.) and

> Some rising Genius sins up to my Song.

(*Epil. to Satires*, Dialogue ii. 9).

[2] *Mor. Ess.* (*Of the Knowledge and Characters of Men*), 228.

[3] *Im. of Hor.* Ep. II. ii. 324–5.

[4] *Ep. to Robert Earl of Oxford*, 31.

[5] *Ep. to Arbuthnot*, 84.

[6] See *Lives of the Poets*, ed. G. Birkbeck Hill, iii. 341, his verses on
Warton, and the parody 'Hermit hoar . . .'.

rules. For all his excitement, he remembers that he is out for

> Something in Verse as true as Prose.[1]

These rules apply unless 'appropriateness' demands their temporary suspension. Pope's own standards are implied in his reply to Lord Hervey. The *Letter to a Noble Lord* is partly an attack on grammar, faulty sense, and wrongly worked out images. What Pope found wanting in Lord Hervey's verse, he sought to supply in his own. The avoidance of poeticisms and attention to the rules of prose order provide further contradictions of the common view that Pope and the eighteenth-century poets were mainly poets of 'poetic diction' and artifice.

Coleridge, in the *Biographia Literaria*, considered that in the satires, Pope was a poet of 'almost faultless position and choice of words', a verdict which, considering the standards Coleridge had already made clear, has more weight than that of any other English critic.[2] One couplet will suffice as example:

> The Stage how loosely does Astræa tread,
> Who fairly puts all Characters to bed![3]

The words in the first line are in unusual order, those of the colloquial second line are not. The first line shows inversion at its simplest and boldest—that of the object and the subject-and-verb. The effect is to tell us that in the discussion of comedy that is proceeding it is Mrs. Behn's plays that are in question,

---

[1] Swift's part of the imitation of Horace's *Satires* II. vi which Pope completed, l. 26.

[2] *Biog. Lit.*, ed. Shawcross, i. 26 n.

[3] *Im. of Hor.* Ep. II. i. To Augustus, 290–1.

not her novels, her capacity to construct dramatic
plots, not narratives. The inversion therefore gives
the sense 'When it is plays that Mrs. Behn is writing
how loose they are—loose in construction as well as in
morals.' Moreover, the inversion helps to produce
the tone of contemptuous exclamation, requiring to
exaggerate its pompous gesture as a contrast to Mrs.
Behn's looseness. This pomp justifies the expletive,
which is here doing anything but 'join' a 'feeble aid'.

VI

Pope's diction in Homer had a special justification. His Postscript to the *Odyssey* was largely a plea
for appropriateness of diction. And yet on the face
of it Pope's language seems anything but appropriate to Homer's. The key to Pope's practice may
be found in certain notes appended to the translation.
The most concise of these notes is that affixed to the
following lines:

> As from fresh pastures and the dewy field
> (When loaded cribs their evening banquet yield)
> The lowing herds return; around them throng
> With leaps and bounds their late-imprison'd young,
> Rush to their mothers with unruly joy,
> And ecchoing hills return the tender cry . . .[1]

The note was probably Broome's but had Pope's
sanction, and derives much of its material and wording from the note to *Iliad*, xi. 669. It reads,

If this simile were to be render'd literally it would run
thus; 'as calves seeing the droves of cows returning at night

[1] x. 485 ff. (I quote the duodecimo edition, 1725).

when they are fill'd with their pasturage, run skipping out
to meet them; the stalls no longer detain them, but running
round their dams they fill the plain with their lowings, &c.'
If a similitude of this nature were to be introduced into
modern Poetry, I am of opinion it would fall under ridicule
for a want of delicacy: but in reality, images drawn from
Nature, and a rural life, have always a very good effect; in
particular, this before us enlivens a melancholy description
of sorrows, and so exactly expresses in every point the joy of
Ulysses's companions, we see them in the very description.
To judge rightly of comparison, we are not to examine if the
subject from whence they are deriv'd be great or little, noble
or familiar, but we are principally to consider if the image
produc'd be clear and lively, if the Poet have skill to dignify
it by Poetical words, and if it perfectly paints the thing it is
intended to represent. This rule fully vindicates *Homer*, tho'
he frequently paints low life, yet he never uses terms which
are not noble; or if he uses humble words or phrases, it is with
so much art, that, as *Dionysius* observes, they become noble
and harmonious: In short, a Top may be used with propriety
and elegance in a similitude by a *Virgil*, and the Sun may
be dishonour'd by a *Maevius*; a mean thought express'd in
noble terms being more tolerable, than a noble thought
disgrac'd by mean expressions . . . it shews the skill of a Poet
to raise a low subject, and exalt common appearances into
dignity.

Homer, that is, employs words which for him were
noble, but of which the modern equivalents are
ignoble. Boileau had pointed this out in his notes
on Longinus, a passage from which is translated and
adapted in Pope's note to *Iliad*, xi. 669.

Thus the word *Asinus* in *Latin*, and *Ass* in *English*, are the
vilest imaginable, but that which signifies the same Animal
in *Greek* and *Hebrew*, is of Dignity enough to be employed

on the most magnificent Occasions. In like manner the Terms of a *Hogherd* and *Cowkeeper* in our Language are insufferable, but those which answer to them in *Greek*... are graceful and harmonious: and *Virgil* who in his own Tongue entitled his Eclogs *Bucolica*, would have been ashamed to have called them in ours, the *Dialogues of Cowkeepers*.

Homer had plainly named an ass in a simile for Ajax, a simile which Pope very much admired. Another portion of the same note reads:

This whole Passage is inimitably just and beautiful, we see *Ajax* drawn in the most bold and strong Colours, and in a manner alive in the Description. We see him slowly and sullenly retreat between two Armies, and even with a Look repulsing the one, and protecting the other: There is not one Line but what resembles *Ajax*; the Character of a stubborn but undaunted Warrior is perfectly maintain'd, and must strike the Reader at the first view. He compares him first to the Lion for his Undauntedness in Fighting, and then to the Ass for his stubborn Slowness in retreating; tho' in the latter Comparison there are many other Points of Likeness that enliven the Image. . . .

The note goes on to show how French critics have allowed Homer the choice of the ass, since asses were dignified animals in those times.[1] But that dignity, it was clear, would be dissipated if a modern western author translated the word literally. For Pope, *ass* was a despised word for a despised object, and, just because of this, a word which he was to

[1] Cf. the note on *Genesis* xlix. 14 (Issachar is a strong ass . . .) in Christopher Wordsworth's Bible (1875) I. i. 193: 'The ass is an animal of much beauty and strength in the East: see Judges v. 10, 2 Sam. xvi. 2, Job xxx. 5.'

use on ten occasions in his satires.[1] Meanwhile he felt the need of periphrasis:

> . . . upon the whole, a Translator owes so much to the Taste of the Age in which he lives, as not to make too great a Compliment to a former; and this induced me to omit the mention of the word *Ass* in the Translation.

He therefore translated the similes both of the lion and of the ass with equal care for dignity:

> Thus the grim Lion his Retreat maintains,
> Beset with watchful Dogs, and shouting Swains,
> Repuls'd by Numbers from the nightly Stalls,
> Tho' Rage impells him, and tho' Hunger calls,
> Long stands the show'ring Darts, and missile Fires;
> Then sow'rly slow th'indignant Beast retires.
> So turn'd stern *Ajax*, by whole Hosts repell'd,
> While his swoln Heart at ev'ry Step rebell'd.
>
> As the slow Beast with heavy Strength indu'd,
> In some wide Field by Troops of Boys pursu'd,
> Tho' round his Sides a wooden Tempest rain,
> Crops the tall Harvest, and lays waste the Plain;
> Thick on his Hide the hollow Blows resound,
> The patient Animal maintains his Ground,
> Scarce from the Field with all their Efforts chas'd,
> And stirs but slowly when he stirs at last.
> On *Ajax* thus a Weight of *Trojans* hung,
> The Strokes redoubled on his Buckler rung. . . .[2]

Even a fly[3] in Homer's language seemed too noble to brook literal translation. In the translation of *Iliad*, xvii. 642 ff. Pope has thought best to call it a vengeful hornet:

---

[1] The figures here and below are derived from E. Abbott's *Concordance.*

[2] 675 ff.   [3] Homer, of course, meant the gad-fly.

So burns the vengeful Hornet (Soul all o'er)
Repuls'd in vain, and thirsty still for Gore;
(Bold Son of Air and Heat) on angry Wings
Untam'd, untir'd, he turns, attacks, and stings:
Fir'd with like Ardour fierce *Atrides* flew,
And sent his Soul with ev'ry Lance he threw.

He notes that there is no 'Impropriety' in the comparison. Flies are what Homer says. But perhaps even flies were more 'dignified' on the plain of Troy than in London.

. . . our present Idea of the Fly is indeed very low, as taken from the Littleness and Insignificancy of this Creature. However, since there is really no Meanness in [Homer's simile] there ought to be none in expressing it.

And so he writes 'vengeful Hornet'. In the *Essay on Man*[1] and the *Dunciad*[2] he does not avoid the word *fly*, and, indeed, among all English poets, he is the one most intently fascinated by small, mean, dirty, idle or 'industrious' insects, all of which he names. While Swift saw the men he hated as animals, Pope saw them as insects. Pope's heightened translation of the fly simile in Homer itself showed how excellently he had observed the hornet which he substituted for the fly. He was offering Homer the best poetry he was capable of, a poetry which did not scruple to save Homer from the accidental differences of modern English connotations.

These problems were discussed specifically in relation to similes. But all through the poem the same principles held good. Pope was throughout engaged in 'transfusing the Spirit of the Original,

[1] i. 194.   [2] iv. 454.

and supporting the Poetical Style of the Translation.'[1] He was helped in supporting the style (he is still thinking of the awful dignity of Homer) by the example of intervening epic poets. In the *Preface* he says outright that a translator of Homer should consider him attentively in comparison with Virgil and Milton. The result of considering Milton may be seen in such a passage as the close of Hephaestos's last speech in the first book. This is translated by Lang, Leaf, and Myers in the following way:

. . . all day I flew, and at the set of sun I fell in Lemnos and little life was in me. There did the Sintian folk forthwith tend me for my fall.

Milton had described the rebel angels as

Hurl'd headlong flaming from th'Ethereal Sky[2]

and he had recalled the incident of Homer's Hephaestos later in the same Book:

. . . he fell

From Heav'n, they fabl'd, thrown by angry *Jove*
Sheer o'er the Chrystal Battlements: from Morn
To Noon he fell, from Noon to dewy Eve,
A Summers day; and with the setting Sun
Dropt from the Zenith like a falling Star,
On *Lemnos* th'*Ægæan* Ile . . .[3]

Pope's version takes its statement from Homer as Milton did but enlarges on it with a remembrance of Milton:

Hurl'd headlong downward from th' Etherial Height;
Tost all the Day in rapid Circles round;
Nor 'till the Sun descended, touch'd the Ground:

---

[1] *Preface*, (folio edition) Sig. H [*1st series*] 1r.
[2] *P.L.* i. 45.   [3] Id. 740 ff.

Breathless I fell, in giddy Motion lost;
The *Sinthians* rais'd me on the *Lemnian* Coast. . . .

Along with the example of Virgil went that of Ovid,
as it had for Dryden. What amounts to a parallel
statement to Pope's about Virgil and Milton is
found in Dryden's preface to his *Aeneid*. Pope
thinks of Virgil and Milton when translating Homer;
Dryden thinks of Ovid. The preface to the *Aeneid*
has some disparaging references to Ovid. Ovid, for
instance, has borrowed Dido from Virgil for his
Heroides and is found to have substituted witticism
for nature. And yet a few lines farther on Dryden is
speaking in Horatian phrase of the 'splendid
miracles' of the *Metamorphoses* and calling them
'beautiful'. The truth is that the technique of Ovid,
whom he had translated plentifully, fascinated
Dryden unduly as a translator of Virgil. This predilection was obvious in the preface as well as in the
translation, and it mainly affects what Dryden called
the 'turn', an 'ornament' of which Ovid was the
consummate master. Dryden discloses his cross-pur-
poses in the discussion of French and English style,
and of Virgil and Ovid:

The French have set up purity for the standard of their
language; and a masculine vigour as that of ours. Like their
tongue is the genius of their poets, light and trifling in comparison of the English; more proper for sonnets, madrigals,
and elegies, than heroic poetry. The turn on thoughts and
words is their chief talent; but the Epic Poem is too stately
to receive those little ornaments. The painters draw their
nymphs in thin and airy habits; but the weight of gold and of
embroideries is reserved for queens and goddesses. Virgil is

never frequent in those turns, like Ovid, but much more sparing of them in his *Æneis* than in his *Pastorals* and *Georgics.*

> Ignoscenda quidem, scirent si ignoscere manes.

That turn is beautiful indeed; but he employs it in the story of Orpheus and Eurydice, not in his great poem. I have used that licence in his *Æneis* sometimes; but I own it as my fault. 'Twas given to those who understand no better. 'Tis like Ovid's

> Semivirumque bovem, semibovemque virum.

The poet found it before his critics, but it was a darling sin, which he would not be persuaded to reform.[1]

In his *Discourse concerning the Original and Progress of Satire* Dryden gives the history of his own acquaintance with the turn. Not until twenty years before, that is, not until the 1670's, had he become aware of 'those beauties which gave the last perfection' to the works of Waller and Denham. Tracing the history of this ornament backwards into earlier poetry he found that it began in Virgil and Ovid.[2] The turn was Ovid's 'darling sin' and, as translators, it was also Dryden's and Pope's. When Dryden translates Virgil he has Ovid in mind. When Pope translates Homer, whom Dryden considers too early a writer to have discovered the turn, he remembers Virgil and Milton, and remembering Virgil means remembering Dryden's Ovidian version which 'notwithstanding some human Errors' is 'the most noble and spirited Translation I know in any Language'.[3]

Dryden's translation of Virgil is much closer to

---

[1] *Ep. Ded. to Aeneis, Essays,* ed. Ker, ii. 219.

[2] *Essays,* ed. Ker, ii. 108 ff.

[3] *Pref.* to *Iliad* (folio edition), Sig. K [1st series] 1r.

his translation of Ovid than Virgil is to Ovid. His translation of Homer is similar in style to his translation of Virgil. Both are Ovidian. Pope's translation belongs to the same group as Dryden's.[1] It therefore draws freely on the linguistic methods and vocabulary that had been associated with verse translations of Latin poetry and with progressive poets of the seventeenth century.

VII

Pope inherited the Elizabethan dread that the English language had a limited future.

> Short is the date, alas, of modern rhymes,
> And 'tis but just to let them live betimes.
> No longer now that golden age appears,
> When Patriarch-wits surviv'd a thousand years:
> Now length of Fame (our second life) is lost,
> And bare threescore is all ev'n that can boast;
> Our sons their fathers' failing language see,
> And such as Chaucer is, shall Dryden be.[2]

Pope returned to the subject again in the Preface to his collected *Works* in 1717:

If we can pretend to have used the same industry [as the Ancients] let us expect the same immortality: Tho' if we took the same care, we should still lie under a farther misfortune: they writ in languages that became universal and everlasting, while ours are extremely limited both in extent and in duration. A mighty foundation for our pride! when the utmost we can hope, is but to be read in one Island, and to be thrown aside at the end of one Age.

As late as 1635 Sir Francis Kinaston had considered

---

[1] See Note p. 172.   [2] *Ess. on Criticism*, 476 ff.

it worth translating two Books of *Troilus and Criseyde* into Latin so as to place it permanently beyond the reach of decay.[1] Waller supported the view in his *Of English Verse*:

> Poets that lasting marble seek
> Must carve in LATIN, or in GREEK:
> We write in sand, our language grows,
> And, like the tide, our work o'er-flows.

Pope's preoccupation with correctness in language is aimed partly at keeping English afloat. His envy of the adamant of Latin led him to respect and extend the seventeenth-century practice of latinizing English. In his early work his respect was shown mainly in vocabulary and methods of phrasing, in the later work mainly in the close Latin-like packing of the line, and the precise correctness of each word used. Correctness was a likely preservative.

In a letter of 18 February 1724, Bolingbroke, glancing back to Pope's 1717 Preface, was more hopeful:

> What! write for fame in a living language which changes every year, and which is hardly known beyond the bounds of our island. Continue to write, and you will contribute to fix it.

It is an ironic commentary on Pope's fear, that even when, in the *Dunciad*, he most risked decay by writing a poem which could not be understood twenty miles from London and which even there looked like being unintelligible at the end of a few

[1] He gives as the first of his reasons for translating: 'conservatio huius poematum gemmæ ab interitu & oblivione . . .' (A 3ᵛ).

years[1] the language of the poem should have preserved as certainly as amber the very

> . . . hairs, or straws, or dirt, or grubs, or worms[2]

of the material.

VIII

To be concise in the meaning and use of words seemed one of the surest ways of preventing the decay of the English language. Pope might have presented the *Essay on Man* in prose, if prose had been, among other things, as concise as verse.[3] In 'measuring [his] syllables and coupling [his] rimes',[4] he would

> show no mercy to an empty line.[5]

Pope makes no fuss about his conciseness, as Browning does. Indeed so still are the waters that their depth is not always noticed. It was partly because of his wish to be concise that Latinate phrases—'fleecy care' and the rest—fascinated him in his early work. But his triumphs of conciseness are not in his Latinate phrases. An early triumph which is characteristic comes at the end of his version of the *Merchant's Tale* of Chaucer and would alone have justified his retelling. May has been seen with the squire in the tree by her old blind husband January who has suddenly been given his sight by

---

[1] Swift in a letter to Pope, 16 July 1728.
[2] *Ep. to Arbuthnot*, 170.
[3] See *The Design* prefixed to the poem.
[4] Letter to Caryll of 13 July 1714.
[5] *Im. of Hor.* Ep. ii. ii. 175.

the fairies. She cleverly explains away what he saw, and Pope concludes with the lines

> Both, pleas'd and bless'd, renew'd their mutual vows,
> A fruitful wife, and a believing spouse.[1]

Nothing could be smoother, pleasanter, quieter, or more pungent. This kind of almost surreptitious conciseness becomes more and more evident in his work. As a late example one might take a line from his version of Donne's second satire, a line for which, as in the instance from Chaucer, he has sole responsibility:

> No rat is rhym'd to death, or maid to love.[2]

Rats, maids, love, death (in the two senses of human dissolution and death *post coitum*) hideously change places. The line is terrifying when, as it must be, it is thought about. As another example of the weight of a single word, there is the line (Pope is speaking of man):

> Of half that live the butcher and the tomb.[3]

But the point scarcely needs illustrating. There are examples on every page. And if he is not actually arresting the reader with the condensed force of single words or groups, he is always writing briefly. The only empty lines in his collected works are those parodying the emptiness of other people's pastorals:

> Of gentle Philips will I ever sing,
> With gentle Philips shall the valleys ring.
> My numbers too for ever will I vary,
> With gentle Budgell and with gentle Carey.
> Or if in ranging of the names I judge ill,
> With gentle Carey and with gentle Budgell. . . .[4]

[1] 815 f.   [2] 22.   [3] *Essay on Man*, iii. 162.
[4] *Three Gentle Shepherds*, 1 ff.

Pope's standards for writing in the heroic couplet are those for writing in other metres. He can, for example, write the tetrameter and trimeter stanza in a way that reminds one of Gray's odes *On the Spring* and *On the Death of a Favourite Cat*:

> Obscure by birth, renown'd by crimes,
> Still changing names, religions, climes,
>   At length she turns a Bride:
> In di'monds, pearls, and rich brocades,
> She shines the first of batter'd jades,
>   And flutters in her pride.
>
> So have I known those Insects fair
> (Which curious Germans hold so rare)
>   Still vary shapes and dyes;
> Still gain new Titles and new forms;
> First grubs obscene, then wriggling worms,
>   Then painted butterflies.[1]

Or there is this, thick with nouns and the solider parts of speech:

> Still idle, with a busy air,
>   Deep whimsies to contrive;
> The gayest valetudinaire,
>   Most thinking rake, alive. . . .
> Luxurious lobster-nights, farewell,
>   For sober, studious days!
> And Burlington's delicious meal,
>   For salads, tarts, and pease![2]

The standards which Pope elected for his major works are virtually those of his minor ones, too. They assemble the least fluid parts of speech and yet escape congestion either of meaning or metre.

---

[1] Imitation of the Earl of Dorset: *Phryne*, 13 ff.
[2] *A Farewell to London*, stanzas 11 and 13.

CORRECTNESS

IV. VERSIFICATION: 'CERTAIN NICETIES'

I

POPE looked back to Dryden as Dryden had looked back to Waller. For Dryden Waller was the most important technical innovator of the seventeenth century. Certain poets before Waller had hit on the closed couplet accidentally. Shakespeare had produced in Iago's speech on women a string of them. Waller in some of his later work had converted this accidental discovery into a system. So well did he do his work that Dryden, when he began writing, found a measure ready waiting. Dryden's work was twice summarized by Pope. The prose summary is found in Spence:

I learned versification wholly from Dryden . . who had improved it much beyond any of our former poets; and would, probably, have brought it to its perfection, had not he been unhappily obliged to write so often in haste.[1]

There was much still to do on the couplet when Pope began to write. Dryden had written it with a knowledge of the compactness of which it was capable, but not always with a realization of that compactness. In some ways he may be said to have helped the measure to revert to a freer form resembling, in rough and ready convenience, the couplets of the Elizabethans.

Dryden avoided the tetrameter (though on occasion

[1] p. 281.

sion he used it superbly) because, as he said, it did
not give him 'room to turn round in'. A poet who
looked on metres as spaces for the cycles of a generous
body was not the poet to discover the final perfection
of the heroic couplet. Dryden found the heroic
couplet, as he found the tetrameter, too small to
turn round in and enlarged it accordingly. He
frequently made it a triplet, especially in his translations, and frequently made the last of the three lines
an alexandrine. He does not seem to have been a
poet who accommodated an unruly thought to metre
by revising the form it had just taken. He was
usually more ready to make space for its completion
in the line following. Sometimes he will write two
triplets on end. Once in the *Aeneid* there are three
on end,[1] and in his version of the *Wife of Bath's
Tale*,[2] five. The triplet is often in Dryden a mark of
slovenliness. On three occasions in his translation of
Virgil's second *Georgic* he begins a new sentence
with the third line of a triplet simply because he
finds a third rime comes conveniently.[3] Triplets have
the undesirable effect of introducing an element of
stanza among the couplets. When, for instance, the
last line of a triplet is, as it often is in Dryden, an
alexandrine, he is writing in the stanza form of
Rochester's *On Nothing*. Dryden has other abnor-
malities than triplet or triplet-with-alexandrine, and,
from the point of view of 'correct' versification, even
more serious ones. For instance, *Against the Fear of*

[1] xi. 925 ff.
[2] 7-21.
[3] ll. 193, 519, 576.

Death, a translation from Lucretius, provides such things as two alexandrines on end and even lines of seven feet.

In his dramatic work, and occasionally elsewhere, Dryden had adopted an innovation which Cowley had made in his *Davideis*. Among the more or less strict couplets of this small epic poem, Cowley had introduced the hemistich, or fragmentary line. He has a note on his innovation:

Though none of the *English Poets*, nor indeed of the ancient *Latin*, have imitated *Virgil* in leaving sometimes half-verses (where the sense seems to invite a man to that liberty) yet his authority alone is sufficient, especially in a thing that looks so naturally and gracefully: and I am far from their opinion who think that *Virgil* himself intended to have filled up those broken *Hemistiques*.[1]

Unlike Virgil, Cowley uses the hemistich only in direct speech—perhaps this is why he considers that it looks naturally. But it certainly does not look gracefully, since, unlike Virgil, Cowley is writing strictly rimed verse. An unrimed and incomplete line when found in the middle of epic couplets has the effect of boxing the reader's ear. Dryden usually avoids this scrap-line in his non-dramatic works—he discusses the point appropriately in his *Dedication of the Aeneis*.[2] In his rimed plays his use of it marks a

[1] Note 14 to Bk. I. Cowley's statement requires the qualification that Ogilby's translation of the *Aeneid* (1649), although a translation into heroic couplets, had preserved Virgil's hemistichs. And Cowley was probably unacquainted with the brief extra-metrical phrases which Marston had inserted among the couplets of his *Scourge of Villanie* (2nd edition 1599). And see note 1, p. 108.

[2] *Essays*, ed. Ker, ii. 230–1.

transitional point between the heroic couplet with
complete lines and blank verse. Dryden was justified
in making his measure more plastic for the purposes
of dramatic speech.[1] Hemistichs may be justified in
drama but Dryden's use of them helped to support
Cowley's unfortunate authority for their use in non-
dramatic poetry. They are frequently used in 'lyric'
work by the small poets of Dryden's and Tonson's
Miscellanies, as, for example, in Henry Cromwell's
translation of an elegy from Ovid's *Amores* in the
Miscellany of 1712:

> The Cow rose slowly from her Consort's Side,
> But when afar the grazing Bull she spy'd,
> Frisk'd to the Herd with an impetuous haste,
> And pleas'd, in new luxuriant Soil, her Taste.
> Oh learn'd Diviner!
> What may this visionary Dream portend,
> If Dreams in any future Truth can end. . . .[2]

Dryden usually justifies his hemistichs. He also
justifies his triplets and alexandrines when he is

---

[1] This was sometimes Shakespeare's practice, though, since Shakespeare's plays are never entirely in couplets, the analogy is not complete.
Having adopted the couplet as a device for closing a scene, he seems to
have half repented of the precision and to have blurred it by adding a
word or two after the rime. *Hamlet* ends with this making and marring
of precision:

Fortinbras . . . Take vp the bodies, such a sight as this,
> Becomes the field, but heere showes much amisse.
> Goe bid the souldiers shoote.

The same device is used brilliantly to close *As You Like It*, I. ii.

Orlando . . . Thus must I from the smoake into the smother.
> From tyrant Duke, vnto a tyrant Brother.
> But heauenly *Rosalind*.

[2] *Miscellaneous Poems* . . ., 1712, p. 116. The last instance of the
hemistich I have noted comes in *The British Coffee-House* [anon.] (1764).

using them for the favourite purpose of onomatopoeia. His triplets and alexandrines are justified
when the idea swells or crescendos along with the
metre. *Absalom and Achitophel,* for example, contains
the couplet:

> Now, free from Earth, thy disencumbered Soul
> Mounts up, and leaves behind the Clouds and Starry Pole.[1]

In his letter to Walsh of 22 October 1706, Pope
enunciated the rules he had come to see valuable for
the writing of couplets. His fourth rule reads:

> I would also object to the irruption of Alexandrine verses,
> of twelve syllables, which, I think, should never be allow'd
> but when some remarkable beauty or propriety . . atones for
> the liberty: Mr. Dryden has been too free of these, especially
> in his latter works. I am of the same opinion as to Triple
> Rhimes.

In the *Essay on Criticism* he mocked at the alexandrine
by comparing it to a wounded snake dragging its
slow length along. But its wounded drag need not
be offensive—the slowness is often a 'remarkable
beauty or propriety'. The real trouble about the
alexandrine, unless it is part of a stanza form as in
the *Faerie Queene*, is the incalculableness of its
'irruption'. The trouble about the alexandrine is that
it begins like an ordinary pentameter and the reader
is somewhere about the middle of the line before he
realizes that the end is an additional foot farther
away. This discovery is often delayed because the
length of a line in type is accidental and so may or
may not represent its length in time. The objection

---

[1] i. 850–1.

to the alexandrine is really that the snake begins like a normal one and only falls heavily stricken somewhere about its middle joint. The triplet was more predictable. It always advertised its approach in the original editions with a heavy marginal bracket. It seems a law, to use the words which Coleridge applied to Shakespeare's dramatic method, that metre should work by expectation rather than by surprise. Dryden's *Against the Fear of Death* is an irritating poem to read. It begins with a long passage of ordinary couplets, lulling the reader into a sense of metrical security, but then proceeds to toss and turn with alexandrines and heptameters. In his versification, Dryden often took the readiest way, trusting, as he had the right to trust, that his mounting rush of sense and sound could bear down all obstacles. His reader acquiesces since such power is a unique phenomenon, but he cannot escape, in a large measure, that nervous sense of insecurity which it is the duty of versification to tranquillize. Any variations, as Pope knew, should be made responsibly. The reader must feel secure.

Pope realized that 'remarkable beauty or propriety' might be provided by the alexandrine and triplet. In his early work he tried to secure such effects. He mimics Dryden, at his most worthy, in his translation of Statius—for example:

> Here all their Rage, and ev'n their Murmurs cease,
> And sacred Silence reigns, and universal peace.[1]

or

[1] ll. 290–1.

> Whence, far below, the Gods at once survey ⎫
> The Realms of rising and declining Day, ⎬
> And all th'extended Space of Earth, and Air, and Sea.[1] ⎭

But as time went on, his standards grew more exclusive. Although the alexandrine and triplet might be justifiable for onomatopoetic reasons, Pope found that the necessary onomatopoeia could be provided for by the strict couplet alone, if enough care were taken. Dryden swelled over into hypermetrics whenever it was easy to do so. Pope has often the same reason but satisfies it without hypermetrics. Pope is relying on the operation of the law which makes difficulties overcome more admirable than difficulties accommodated. Examples come everywhere. One has only to look at the close of the *Dunciad* to see how many Drydenian triplets and alexandrines its pentameter couplets avoid.

In the *Epistle to Augustus* Pope summarizes the history of seventeenth-century versification. His tribute to Dryden takes the form of a recreation of the 'darling sin', the triplet-with-alexandrine. (The placing of epithets and the run of the syntax make the mimicry complete.) Pope is thinking of Dryden as an 'incorrect' versifier who nevertheless carries off his effect splendidly—but as the conclusion of the passage shows, not always.

> . . . Numbers learn'd to flow.
> Waller was smooth; but Dryden taught to join ⎫
> The varying verse,[2] the full-resounding line, ⎬
> The long majestic March, and Energy divine. ⎭

---

[1] ll. 277-9.
[2] Pope is thinking of the Pindarique odes.

Tho' still some traces of our rustic vein
And splay-foot verse, remain'd, and will remain.
Late, very late, correctness grew our care,
When the tir'd Nation breath'd from civil war.
Exact Racine, and Corneille's noble fire,
Show'd us that France had something to admire.
Not but the Tragic spirit was our own,
And full in Shakespear, fair in Otway shone:
But Otway fail'd to polish or refine,
And fluent Shakespear scarce effac'd a line.
Ev'n copious Dryden wanted, or forgot,
The last and greatest Art, the Art to blot.[1]

Content apart, Dryden had not advanced the heroic couplet much beyond Waller, except in the matter of onomatopoetic versification. In some ways he had pushed it back. Pope's short history of English versification in the seventeenth century does not state his own position, but implies it.

II

As a boy, Pope was advised by Walsh to be the first 'correct' English poet. So far as Walsh, or he, had versification in mind, they meant correctness in writing the heroic couplet.

The couplet was the important measure for these poets principally because of its unpretentious 'elegance', a quality essential for anything intended to contribute to the pleasure of a cultured society. (*The Spectator* thought that 'the chief Qualification of a good Poet, especially of one who writes Plays' is to be 'a very well-bred Man'.)[2] Blank verse was suitable for epic or tragedy 'where transcendencies are more

[1] ll. 266 ff.   [2] No. 314.

allowed'. The new good poets allowed theoretical supremacy to epic and tragedy—with Aristotle before their eyes they could do no less—but they did their best work in the meaner, more pleasant, and well-bred forms. Pope is always laughing at bad poets who attempt the sublime. The couplet was a measure which did not embarrass the reader, did not make him feel that the poet was giving himself airs. Dryden generally uses the couplet.

> And this unpolish'd, rugged Verse I chose;
> As fittest for Discourse, and nearest prose.[1]

This is in explanation of the verse of the argumentative *Religio Laici*. He chose a more polished style of the couplet for his translations. As early as 1664, in the *Epistle Dedicatory of the Rival Ladies*, he argued the supremacy of rimed verse when written, as Waller had written it, with 'easy' art.

III

In attempting correct versification, therefore, the work of Milton, their revered and immediate predecessor, offered little help. Pope knew Milton's poems thoroughly and admired them to the point of echoing them frequently. But the system of blank verse in *Paradise Lost*, or of other verse elsewhere, had little he wished to copy. Indeed Milton's versification was not considered correct. Even for so late a critic as Johnson, Milton as a metrist is to be excused on the ground that he came too early to profit by the improvements of Dryden—in the same

[1] *Religio Laici*, 453-4.

way that Homer is excused by Dryden for coming too early to profit by the Roman poets' discovery of the 'turn'. Johnson expressed himself clearly on this point in his *Life of John Philips*:

Deformity is easily copied; and whatever there is in Milton which the reader wishes away, all that is obsolete, peculiar, or licentious is accumulated with great care by Philips. Milton's verse was harmonious, in proportion to the general state of our metre in Milton's age, and, if he had written after the improvements made by Dryden, it is reasonable to believe that he would have admitted a more pleasing modulation of numbers into his work. . . .[1]

And even for such an ardent Miltonian as Thomas Warton the younger, it is the 'perspicuous and simple style' of *At a solemn Music* that he admires.[2] Milton was considered unfortunate in coming too early to write correctly, and Dryden did not scruple to 'versify' some of the blank verse of *Paradise Lost* in his *State of Innocence*. When Pope did write blank verse his master was Rowe. This may be seen in the surviving lines of his *Brutus* or wherever he versifies a passage of wrongly alined prose in his edition of Shakespeare. He told Spence that 'Milton's style, in his Paradise Lost, is not natural; 'tis an exotic style'.[3] Pope sees, however, that its uncouthness is appropriate for parts of the poem:

As [Milton's] subject lies a good deal out of our world, [his style] has a particular propriety in those parts of the poem.

It is because of this that his exotic style can be

[1] *Lives*, ed. G. Birkbeck Hill, i. 318.
[2] See L. C. Martin, *Thomas Warton and the Early Poems of Milton* (1934), 17.   [3] p. 174.

'borne'.[1] Atterbury, who greatly admired Milton, suggested that Pope should 'translate' *Samson Agonistes* into correct versification and so provide English poets with a totally correct model for tragedy:

I hope you won't utterly forget what pass'd in the coach about Samson Agonistes. I shall not press you as to time, but some time or other, I wish you would review, and polish that piece. If upon a new perusal of it . . . you think as I do, that it is written in the very spirit of the Ancients; it deserves your care, and is capable of being improved, with little trouble, into a perfect model and standard of Tragic poetry— always allowing for its being a story taken out of the Bible; which is an objection that at this time of day, I know, is not to be got over.[2]

The correct versification which Atterbury foresaw may have been in heroic couplets, though six years earlier he mentioned having held for thirty years the heresy that blank verse is the superior metre.[3]

IV

The value of correctness in or out of the heroic couplet lies first of all in the effect it has on the reader's attitude. When a reader finds that his poet considers himself responsible for every syllable not simply in this or that poem but in every poem of his entire works, then his alertness is intensified, his curiosity aroused, his trust increased. Here, he sees, is a poet who will set him in a motion which will only change as a dance changes, not as a walk on

[1] Id. 200.   [2] Letter of 15 June 1722.
[3] Letter of Dec. 1716.

ice changes. Correctness elicits and does not abuse
the reader's confidence. The reader will, however,
soon tire if nothing happens to show how strong his
confidence is. Once he can trust his poet, he looks
to have the steadfastness of his trust proved and
deepened by variety of experience. Pope satisfies
this expectation in a thousand ways. Pope's practice
is to provide expectation rather than surprise. But
the expectation is expectation *of* surprise. The reader
of Pope anticipates perfect responsibility syllable by
syllable, and awaits the changes which will show that
the responsibility is being put to advantage. The
thousand surprises come and they enchant all the
more because, as certainly as rime in a known stanza,
they have been subconsciously anticipated.

V

Some of the principles upon which Pope worked
in the heroic couplet were enunciated in letters to
Cromwell and Walsh, and most particularly in the
letter to Walsh already mentioned. This letter is the
fulfilment, as are so many other things in Pope,
of a scheme of Dryden's. In the *Dedication to the
Aeneis* he wrote:

I have long had by me the materials of an English *Prosodia*,
containing all the mechanical rules of versification, wherein
I have treated, with some exactness, of the feet, the quantities,
and the pauses.[1]

Pope was also indebted to the excellent preface by
Atterbury to the posthumous second part of Waller's
Poems (1690). Pope's letter to Walsh is written

[1] *Essays*, ed. Ker, ii. 217.

when he is nineteen years old, and it embodies what he had by that time come to realize about English versification from his reading in English and other languages and from his already voluminous practice in writing. The rules were applied in the *Pastorals*, but not so completely in the more difficult poems which followed. The practice, however, fully catches up to the precept by the time these poems appear in the collected *Works* of 1717. Pope writes:

... There are indeed certain Niceties, which, tho' not much observed even by correct versifiers, I cannot but think, deserve to be better regarded.

1. It is not enough that nothing offends the ear, but a good poet will adapt the very Sounds, as well as Words, to the things he treats of. So that there is (if one may express it so) a Style of Sound. As in describing a gliding stream, the numbers should run easy and flowing; in describing a rough torrent or deluge, sonorous and swelling, and so of the rest. This is evident everywhere in Homer and Virgil, and no where else that I know of, to any observable degree. . . . This, I think, is what very few observe in practice, and is undoubtedly of wonderful force in imprinting the image on the reader: We have one excellent example of it in our language, Mr. Dryden's Ode on St. Cæcilia's day, entitled, *Alexander's Feast.*

2. Every nice ear must (I believe) have observ'd, that in any smooth English verse of ten syllables, there is naturally a *Pause* at the fourth, fifth, or sixth syllable. It is upon these the ear rests, and upon the judicious change and management of which depends the variety of versification. For example, At the fifth.

Where'er thy navy | spreads her canvas wings,
At the fourth.

Homage to thee | and peace to all she brings.

At the sixth.

Like tracts of leverets | in morning snow.

Now I fancy, that, to preserve an exact Harmony and Variety, the Pause at the 4th or 6th should not be continued above three lines together, without the interposition of another; else it will be apt to weary the ear with one continued tone, at least it does mine: That at the fifth runs quicker, and carries not quite so dead a weight, so tires not so much, tho' it be continued longer.

3. Another nicety is in relation to Expletives, whether words or syllables, which are made use of purely to supply a vacancy: *Do* before verbs plural is absolutely such; and it is not improbable but future refiners may explode *did* and *does* in the same manner, which are almost always used for the sake of rhime . . .

[For 4 see above, p. 109.]

5. I could equally object to the Repetition of the same Rhimes within four or six lines of each other, as tiresome to the ear thro' their Monotony.

6. Monosyllable Lines, unless very artfully managed, are stiff, or languishing: but may be beautiful to express Melancholy, Slowness, or Labour.

7. To come to the Hiatus, or Gap between two words, which is caus'd by two vowels opening on each other. . . . I think the rule in this case is either to use the Cæsura [by which Pope meant the elision of one of the vowels] or admit the Hiatus, just as the ear is least shock'd by either: For the Cæsura sometimes offends the ear more than the Hiatus itself, and our language is naturally overcharg'd with consonants: As for example; If in the verse,

The old have Int'rest ever in their eye,

we should say, to avoid the Hiatus,

But th'old have Int'rest.

. . . To conclude, I believe the Hiatus should be avoided with more care in poetry than in Oratory; and I would constantly try to prevent it, unless where the cutting it off is more prejudicial to the sound than the Hiatus itself.[1]

Pope's first point is the need for onomatopoeia. In his own work he misses no opportunity where its effects would be appropriate. Pope was following Dryden among the English poets. Dryden had achieved memorable effects of movement, thunder and space, that is, large effects which he could turn round in. Pope has these large effects, but has minute and subtle ones too. The onomatopoetic effects in Pope must be considered as a part of the total elaborate formality of sound, as alternating or coalescing with effects such as balance and inversion. This means that they are not effects erupting from the surface of a poem otherwise careless of formal sound, but effects of equal exactness to those with which they coincide or change places.

Onomatopoeia is a childish effect if it is carried to the extent to which, for instance, Tennyson carried it in the *Idylls*. So ding'd with consonants is a tournament in the *Idylls* that the sounds predominate over the sense. They invite a standard of judgement which is not literary but sonoral. One is made to test the words as an adjudicator at a musical festival would test sound. In his tournaments Tennyson seems to be expecting to produce the actual sounds, rather than to suggest them. The result is that instead of an effect of the deafening clash of real armour against armour, he provides a tintinnabulation which reminds one of the clockwork tournament in Wells Cathedral.

[1] Quoted from Warburton's edition (1753), vii. 49–53.

If one neglects Pope's Homer, it would be fair to both Pope and Tennyson to place Tennyson's

> The moan of doves in immemorial elms

beside Pope's

> With all the mournful family of Yews.[1]

In the first place Tennyson is characteristically trying to produce actual sounds, whereas Pope is translating into mournful sound a mournful visual effect. Moreover, in Pope the line, though serious in itself, is intended in its context to have a comic effect. Pope is amused at the changing fashions in gardens:

> Thro' his young Woods how pleas'd Sabinus stray'd,
> Or sat delighted in the thick'ning shade,
> With annual joy the redd'ning shoots to greet,
> Or see the stretching branches long to meet!
> His Son's fine Taste an op'ner Vista loves,
> Foe to the Dryads of his Father's groves;
> One boundless Green, or flourish'd Carpet views,
> With all the mournful family of Yews;
> The thriving plants ignoble broomsticks made,
> Now sweep those Alleys they were born to shade.

The content of Pope's line is more satisfactory than that of Tennyson's, more valuable as poetry than *immemorial elms*. The image of a dove in an elm tree is not so good as the line is musical. Elm trees are whiskery and coarse trees unless seen at a distance, and at a distance the moan of their doves would be inaudible. This happens with the line, if one neglects the music. In practice one cannot neglect the music. It is much too potent. But the result is that the elm trees are not real ones. The line makes

[1] *Mor. Essays*, iv. To Burlington, 96.

one suspend the working of the brain and accept sounds instead. This is a too ready magic, for a great poet. Pope does not allow music to smother sense and his line is the finer because of it. *Mournful family of yews* brings out qualities that are actually there in yews. Pope writes, as Wordsworth counselled, with his eye on the object, and so his ear is kept in its right place, of its right size. Tennyson shuts his eye and extends an ear like a gramophone horn. He shows himself as a Liszt *manqué*, not as an artist in words. There is no need to give examples of Pope's 'beautiful' onomatopoetic effects—most of the examples of description in Chapter One would serve to show how far from childish they are. Pope is frequently not so much echoing sound in sound as equating a visual impression with sound. Many of his onomatopoetic effects are comic ones—onomatopoeia was, he saw, a great sharpener of the satiric weapon. And so there come lines like

And the high dome re-echoes to his nose[1]

With gun, drum, trumpet, blunderbuss, and thunder[2]

Yet let me flap this bug with gilded wings,
This painted child of dirt, that stinks and stings[3]

or a hundred examples in the *Dunciad*.

Pope's distinction between *do* before verbs plural and *did* and *does* before verbs singular is due to the conditions of grammar. If a poet wishes to rime the verb 'play' with 'day' and to use it as a plural of

---

[1] *Rape of the Lock*, v. 86.
[2] *Im. of Hor*. Sat. II. i. To Mr. Fortescue, 26.
[3] *Epist. to Arbuthnot*, 309–10.

the present tense, the rime is achieved as easily without an expletive as with one. Instead of ending his
line with 'the boys do play', he can as easily end it with
'the young boys play'. But if the word which has to
have a rime found for it is still 'day', and the subject
of the convenient rime 'play' happens to be singular,
then the poet, who is prevented by grammar from
'the boy play', can be allowed to write 'the boy does
play'. But Pope came to be numbered among the
'future refiners' at the latest by 1717. The many
revised poems in the *Works* of this year, as well as
the few new poems, mark together a great technical
advance. In the edition of the *Rape of the Lock* in
this volume there are several verbal changes, four
of which affect passages which contain the word *did*.

> *Sol* thro' white Curtains did his Beams display,
> (1712)

becomes

> *Sol* thro' white curtains shot a tim'rous ray,[1]
> (1717)

> Steel did the Labour of the Gods destroy,
> And strike to Dust th'aspiring Tow'rs of *Troy*;
> (1712)

becomes 'Steel could . . .' in 1717: ('th'aspiring' had
been changed to 'th'Imperial' in 1714.)[2]

> 'Twas this, the morning *Omens* did foretel[l];

becomes ' . . . seem'd to tell;' in 1717.[3]

> See the poor Remnants of this slighted Hair!
> My hands shall rend what ev'n thy own did spare.
> (1712)

---

[1] i. 13.   [2] iii. 173-4.   [3] iv. 161.

becomes

> See the poor remnants of these slighted hairs!
> My hands shall rend what ev'n thy rapine spares;
>
> (1717)[1]

These rules drawn up by the young Pope are simple, of course, in comparison with the methods of Pope's mature work. The second rule, for example, shows almost naïvely against the controlled complexity of the couplets in the satires and the *Dunciad*. There are no rules which would adequately cover the later couplets except the philosophic ones which relate difficult matter to style. One or two simplicities, however, may be noted. Pope prefers almost to the point of insistence that the rime word should be monosyllabic. In the *Rape of the Lock* only three couplets have feminine rimes. These feminine rimes are all intended for particular effects. This is universally true of his rimes. The rime-word is therefore almost always stressed.

Shenstone enunciated a subsidiary rule for him:

> Rhymes, in elegant poetry, should consist of syllables that are long in pronunciation; such as *are, ear, ire, ore, your*; in which a nice ear will find more agreeableness than in these *gnat, net, knit, knot, nut*.[2]

Richard Mant considered Dryden responsible for faulty rimes in Thomas Warton the younger:

> He seems to have copied Dryden, perhaps not always judiciously, in one respect; in terminating a verse with a trisyllable, which will hardly bear the accent, where it will then of necessity be, on the last syllable; and in making the

---

[1] Id. 167–8.
[2] *On Writing and Books*, maxim XL.

verse so formed the leading verse of the couplet. Thus in
the Triumph of Isis,

> Like Greece in science and in libertỳ,
> As Athens learn'd, as Lacedæmon free.

And in Verses to Sir Joshua Reynolds,

> With arts unknown before to reconcìle
> The willing Graces to the Gothic pile.[1]

Shenstone stated his rule in its strictest form. Pope
finds occasion to depart from it, but, when he does
so, he is conscious of the departure. And the rime
on a weak syllable is rare, but does occur:

> Her Priestless Muse forbids the Good to die,
> And opes the Temple of *Eternity*[2]

(though here, it must be remembered, Pope is
quoting almost verbatim from *Comus*).

All through his work Pope seems to have preferred
a verb for at least one of the rime-words in a couplet.
This was a means of attaining a full stress for the
rime. A verb at the end of the first line is often
followed by its object in the next line. This provided
the couplet with bipartite unity instead of with
unified duality.

VI

The rules to Walsh touch on but do not go into
the most important characteristic of Pope's versification, its skill in effects of balance. (This matter
is not, of course, one wholly of versification: it concerns syntax and meaning itself.) Pope's simplest
effects of balance may be studied in the *Pastorals*, in

---

[1] *The Poetical Works of . . . Thomas Warton* (1802), I. cxxxi.
[2] *Epil. to Sat.* Dial. ii. 234-5.

which, of all his poems, the versification had been
most 'laboured' into correctness.[1] The following
examples are not to be regarded as 'types'. It is best,
when studying versification, to consider that there
is no such thing as a 'type' of line. Lines may
resemble each other in structure, but each line in
poetry should be seen as a unique phenomenon.
Pope of course does not 'invent' many of the patterns; his poems are remarkable for their combination of so many varieties of the patterns and in their
control of that combination.

(1) The mossy fountains, and the green retreats!
                                        (*Summer*, 72)

This line of virtually four stresses is fairly common,
and had been used on several memorable occasions
—for example by Sidney:

A rosie garland, and a wearie head.[2]

Pope's fondness for this kind of line has been noted
by Bridges in his *Milton's Prosody*.[3]

(2) But often Pope provides an antithesis as well
as an echo. For example,

So sweetly warble, or so smoothly flow
                                        (*Winter*, 4)

where each adverb is so placed as to balance the
other with comparison or contrast. Effects of which
these are the simplest examples were favourites with
Pope. The late seventeenth century may be said to
have discovered their fascination. Shakespeare, for
example, sometimes went out of his way to avoid the

---

[1] Spence, 312.   [2] *Astrophel and Stella*, xxxix. 11.
[3] Ed. 1901, p. 14.

maximum balance. The last eight lines of *King Lear*
form four couplets and the last but one of these reads:

> The waight of this sad time we must obey,
> Speake what we feele, not what we ought to say.

The meaning of this line would have been more
correctly expressed if the verbs, which are identical
in meaning, had been identical in sound. There is
no antithesis between *speak* and *say*, the antithesis is
between *feel* and *ought*. Shakespeare obscures this
by employing two different verbs, each with the
meaning of *say*. This is the kind of 'elegant variation'
which Yeats found to dislike in the prose of Wilde.
Pope would have written that line as

> Say what we feel, not what we ought to say.

And this is the natural way the line should run.
Shakespeare here avoids making the clauses echo
each other as exactly as possible, even though this
helps his meaning.

(3) Sometimes there is balance between two unequal parts:

> With Waller's strains, and Granville's moving lays.
> (*Spring*, 46)

This uneven balance tends to draw attention to what
causes the unevenness. In this instance, therefore,
moving has particular force.

(4) This unequal balance is capable of variation,
as, for example:

> More bright than noon, yet fresh as early day.
> (*Spring*, 82)

(5) Two Swains, whom Love kept wakeful, and the Muse.
> (*Spring*, 18)

This indicates the ease with which a statement can qualify for treatment in balanced form. There is no antithesis between the swains, although they are two. But their sleep is troubled by two things and these are so used as to make balance possible.

(6) Another instance of unequal balance from the *Pastorals* is

> Fields ever fresh, and groves for ever green,
> *(Winter,* 72)

where the latter half is longer and heavier. (Its alliteration is not only heavier and more complete than the *f* and *fr* of the first half, but is also more widely spaced because of the additional *for.*)

(7) So far the examples have been simple balance or parallels. But the line once divided lent itself as easily to inversion as to parallel. There is this line in the *Pastorals*:

> Fresh as the morn, and as the season fair.
> *(Spring,* 20)

This example shows an inversion of music but not an inversion of meaning: the half-lines are parallel in meaning but inverted in music.

(8) The following is one example of the many variations possible:

> Feed fairer flocks, or richer fleeces shear,
> *(Summer,* 36)

The two verbs are placed at either end of the line and have the same vowel (and that a long one). And there is the further close-knitting provided by the *fl* alliteration of the two nouns.

(9) The principle of inverted echo without antithesis is applied over an entire couplet in:

> Thro' rocks and caves the name of Delia sounds,
> Delia, each cave and echoing rock rebounds.

(Autumn, 49-50)

Rocks . . . caves . . . Delia . . . Delia . . . cave . . . rock.
And then the rime with its effect not of inversion
but of parallel. Here although the meaning literally
concerns echoes (i.e. parallel noises) Pope prefers to
invert the music and so clash that inversion against
the parallel sense.

(10) This system of balances and inversions can
be much more complicated. For example, *January
and May* 742-3, reads:

> 'Tis truth I tell, tho' not in phrase refin'd;
> Tho' blunt my tale, yet honest is my mind.

Here there are two major relationships involving
minor ones: (*a*) the first line balances the second;
and (*b*) the second line inverts the first, so that the
first half of the first line balances the second half of
the second, and the second half of the first line
balances the first half of the second.

(11) Sometimes the line is balanced about a point
deferred until the end, or until near the end:

> Now leaves the trees, and flow'rs adorn the ground.

(Spring, 43)

or

> Nor plains at morn, nor groves at noon delight.

(Spring, 80)

or

> This mourn'd a faithless, that an absent Love.

(Autumn, 3)

This kind of balance about a deferred pivot gains in importance when it is found to link itself to a common effect in Pope. As in Latin poetry, phrases may in themselves seem nonsense and in English also seem ungrammatical, and yet, when read in their context, be found to catch up between their tightly packed constituents the additions needed to relate them into sense. For instance, the phrase 'to their improper, Ill' would be a puzzle on its own. In its context the pause of the comma represents the equivalent of two words which make sense of it:

> Two principles in human nature reign;
> Self-love, to urge, and Reason, to restrain;
> Nor this a good, nor that a bad we call,
> Each works its end, to move or govern all:
> And to their proper operation still,
> Ascribe all Good; to their improper, Ill.[1]

The reader takes pleasure in supplying for himself the rest of the construction by an exercise of memory. This is the kind of way he has to read Latin, though in Latin the case endings make his task easier. It is possible for Pope to place reliance on this prehensile activity with syntax which he has trained his reader to supply. An ambiguity of grammar which would be fairly serious in some authors becomes almost clarity in him. The realization that, in the following couplet, 'turns away' is a transitive verb comes readily since the reader is on the watch for such requirements:

> But Britain, changeful as a Child at play,
> Now calls in Princes, and now turns away.[2]

[1] *Essay on Man*, ii. 53 ff.
[2] *Im. of Hor.* Ep. II. i. To Augustus, 155–6.

Or

> Celestial Venus haunts Idalia's groves;
> Diana Cynthus, Ceres Hybla loves.
>
> *(Spring,* 65-6)

Or

> Years following years, steal something ev'ry day,
> At last they steal us from ourselves away;
> In one our Frolics, *one Amusements end,*
> In one a Mistress drops, in one a Friend.[1]

VII

Pope's regard for versification which, to speak approximately, began in the cause of music and continued in the cause of meaning, was a major element in his effect and his effectiveness. Without this correctness, his other kinds of correctness would have been insignificant. The musical formality of the *Pastorals* taught the readers of Pope's poetry that here was a poet who weighed every letter of his verse. Like the gnomes with the snuff he was 'to ev'ry atom just'. After this exhibition, Pope could be certain of having the requisite attention paid to his effects. And, especially in his later, his consummate, work, it was in full knowledge of this preparedness on the part of his readers that Pope played as if magically with his couplets. It has always been acknowledged that Pope's skill with them was magical or devilish and his importance as a poet has sometimes been left at that. His genius has sometimes been regarded as one expressing itself fully in the supersensitive surface of his technique. But the

[1] *Im. of Hor.* Ep. II. ii. 72 ff.

truth is that this triumph in technique is the counter-part, and no more than that, of a triumph of content. The *Pastorals* draw on a fund of meaning which every poet can draw on without dust or heat. School-boys can as readily decorate the pages of their institutional magazines. But the same measure in the satires, burned out of its lacquered placidity and then frozen again into metal,[1] is the medium for a vision of men and things which is as elaborate as intense. So malleable are its twenty syllables that the couplet never stereotypes the vision. It may some-times help the vision to its sharpness, in the same way that Dryden said rime sometimes helped him to a thought. Pope may sometimes have changed his manner of seeing men when he began to put what he saw into his couplets. One does not know where more praise is owing, for the vision or the verse. Their interaction may well be equal and opposite. By the time the poem has reached the reader there is no indication which pull was the stronger.

With this as preface one can look at some of the effects of the later use of the couplet. Pope has schooled his readers to expect some particular neat effect of balance or antithesis, if not in every line, at least in every couplet. Having set this standard of uniformity in importance, he proceeds to upset it

[1] Cf. Bevil Higgons, *To Mr. Pope* in *Poems on Several Occasions*, 1717 (*Pope's Own Miscellany*, ed. N. Ault, 81):

> Thy wit in vain the feeble Critick gnaws;
> While the hard metal breaks the serpent's jaws.

After Pope, the other satirists of the century seem to wield an axe of wood, however well they have polished and shaped it.

in a hundred ways. He is utilizing to the full the
privilege that for the first poet began with metre,
the privilege of variety when once uniformity has
been established. It would be impossible to cite
every example of his skill. The volumes of his
collected poems do that. Take this passage from the
ending of the *Epistle to Augustus*:

> Not with such majesty, such bold relief,
> The Forms august, of King, or conqu'ring Chief,
> E'er swell'd on marble; as in verse have shin'd
> (In polish'd verse) the Manners and the Mind.
> Oh! could I mount on the Mæonian wing,
> Your Arms, your Actions, your repose to sing!
> What seas you travers'd, and what fields you fought!
> Your Country's peace, how oft, how dearly bought!
> How barb'rous rage subsided at your word,
> And Nations wonder'd while they dropp'd the sword!
> How, when you nodded, o'er the land and deep,
> Peace stole her wing, and wrapt the world in sleep;
> 'Till earth's extremes your mediation own,
> And Asia's Tyrants tremble at your Throne—
> But Verse, alas! your Majesty disdains;
> And I'm not us'd to Panegyric strains;
> The Zeal of Fools offends at any time,
> But most of all, the Zeal of Fools in rhyme.
> Besides, a fate attends on all I write,
> That when I aim at praise, they say I bite.
> A vile Encomium doubly ridicules:
> There's nothing blackens like the ink of fools.
> If true, a woeful likeness: and if lies,
> 'Praise undeserv'd is scandal in disguise':
> Well may he blush, who gives it, or receives;
> And when I flatter, let my dirty leaves

> (Like Journals, Odes, and such forgotten things
> As Eusden, Philips, Settle, writ of Kings)
> Clothe spice, line trunks, or flutt'ring in a row,
> Befringe the rails of Bedlam and Soho.[1]

In this passage the first two couplets form together
one unit, divided after *marble*. The latter part of that
unit has to provide weight enough in its one and a
half lines to balance the two and a half lines of the
former part. This balance Pope manages to achieve,
because of the iron emphasis he places on *in verse*,
an emphasis reinforced by (*In polish'd verse*). His
meaning requires that emphasis and the couplets
are arranged so as to require it, too. This is their
broad outline. One can further note that the second
part itself manages to engineer two sets of balance.
And the second line of the first couplet has two
pauses each marking the limits of the balanced
phrases. What lies between, i.e., ', of King,' is the
pivot. Usually the pivot of a balanced line is a pause
or a subdued stress. Here it is a phrase of two words.
That is the account of the line as music. But as
meaning the balance is between this two-word
phrase and the phrase forming the rest of the line
as one reads forward. Music and meaning are here
two contraries locked in one embrace. There are
other effects, of alliteration (*m* and *k*) and onomatopoeia (the roundness of *swell'd* and the brightness
of *shin'd*). At line six the rising line drops suddenly
to bathos,

> Your Arms, your Actions, your repose . . .

[1] *Im. of Hor.* Ep. II. i. To Augustus, 390 ff.

That bathos was all the more complete since the cultivated reader would be thrown off his guard by remembering Pomfret's line in *Cruelty and Lust*:

> Your Sword, your Conduct, and your Cause attend.[1]

Line seven leisurely blows its twin balloons of wonder, while line eight reserves the huge task of bathos to its last two words. *Dearly bought* changes the whole apparent compliment which preceded, and *oft* which had formerly seemed congratulatory strikes in retrospect its own defamatory blow. There is nothing technically important in the next four couplets. In the couplet following,

> The Zeal of Fools offends at any time,
> But most of all, the Zeal of Fools in rhyme.

the balance—as far as music goes—completes itself by the end of the fourth foot of the last line, so that the remnant, *in rhyme*, which completes the balance of meaning, breaks like a shot from a gun. The last but two of the couplets is broken in half. Its first line finishing off what has been progressing through the last five couplets, its second line beginning, as if from zero, the rise which proceeds like the perpendicular mounting of an aeroplane to a point marked by *trunks* from which summit begins the descent into silence. It is difficult to see what Wordsworth meant when he described Pope's couplets as 'too timidly balanced'.[2]

The above passage may be taken as an ordinary sample of Pope's couplets in the satires. There is

---

[1] *Poems*, ed. 1736, 69.
[2] Letter to Dyce, May 1830.

no end to his variety. He can break them into small
fragments:

> Shut, shut the door, good John! fatigu'd, I said,
> Tie up the knocker, say I'm sick, I'm dead.
> The Dog-star rages! nay 'tis past a doubt,
> All Bedlam, or Parnassus, is let out . . .[1]

Or this dialogue of barks:

> F. . . . Spare then the Person, and expose the Vice.
> P. How, Sir? not damn the Sharper, but the Dice?
> Come on then, Satire! gen'ral, unconfin'd,
> Spread thy broad wing, and souse on all the kind.
> Ye Statesmen, Priests, of one Religion all!
> Ye Tradesmen vile, in Army, Court, or Hall,
> Ye Rev'rend Atheists—F. Scandal! name them! Who?
> P. Why that's the thing you bid me not to do.
> Who starv'd a Sister, who foreswore a Debt,
> I never nam'd; the Town's enquiring yet.
> The pois'ning Dame—F. You mean—P. I don't.—
>   F. You do!
> P. See, now I keep the Secret, and not you![2]

Or this, in which the antithesis straddles over two
and a half lines, the pivotal point taking up the odd
half line in the middle:

> If, when the more you drink, the more you crave,
> You tell the Doctor; when the more you have,
> The more you want; why not with equal ease
> Confess as well your Folly, as Disease?[3]

Pope sometimes varies the structure of the
couplet by placing a normal line partly in the first

---

[1] *Ep. to Arbuthnot*, 1 ff.
[2] *Epil. to Sat.* Dial. ii. 12 ff.
[3] *Im. of Hor.* Ep. ii. 2. 212 ff.

half of the couplet and partly in the second. For example

> In vain, in vain—the all-composing Hour
> Resistless falls: the Muse obeys the Pow'r.[1]

Here 'In vain, in vain, the Muse obeys the Pow'r' and 'the all-composing Hour resistless falls' are normal lines. But their normality is complicated, since the first one has its two component parts severed by the placing of a complete pentameter between them, and the second is broken into unequal sections by coming up against the rime-word. Pope used balance and inversion when he wanted them.   He used a less geometrical line when he wanted that:

> Eyes the calm Sun-set of thy various Day[2]

> Lull with Amelia's liquid name the Nine[3]

> Coffee, (which makes the politician wise,
> And see thro' all things with his half-shut eyes)[4]

> And Shadwell nods the Poppy on his brows[5]

> And universal Darkness buries All.[6]

The undecorated smoothness of such lines is all the smoother for the reader's release from the pointed style either of the immediate or the general context. Pope, like Milton, found such lines were demanded by the architecture of the paragraph.

---

[1] *Dunc.* iv. 627–8.
[2] *Epistle to Robert, Earl of Oxford,* 38.
[3] *Im. of Hor.* Sat. ii. i. To Mr. Fortescue, 31.
[4] *Rape of the Lock,* iii. 117–18.
[5] *Dunc.* iii. 22.
[6] Id. iv. 656.

In the *Essay on Criticism* and much more in the
Essay on Man Pope is using what amounts almost to
a different kind of heroic couplet. The couplets of
the *Essay on Man* bound on feathered heels. Pope
is seldom so easy to read as Dryden, whose verses
are sometimes too glib. But he attains something of
Dryden's speed in this poem. The following is a
fair sample:

> Whate'er the Passion, knowledge, fame, or pelf,
> Not one will change his neighbour with himself.
> The learn'd is happy nature to explore,
> The fool is happy that he knows no more;
> The rich is happy in the plenty giv'n,
> The poor contents him with the care of Heav'n.
> See the blind beggar dance, the cripple sing,
> The sot a hero, lunatic a king;
> The starving chemist in his golden views
> Supremely blest, the poet in his Muse.[1]

The concluding invocation to Bolingbroke adapts
this style to as light a lyric as Pope ever shows:

> Come then, my Friend! my Genius! come along;
> Oh master of the poet, and the song!
> And while the Muse now stoops, or now ascends,
> To Man's low passions, or their glorious ends,
> Teach me, like thee, in various nature wise,
> To fall with dignity, with temper rise;
> Form'd by thy converse, happily to steer
> From grave to gay, from lively to severe;
> Correct with spirit, eloquent with ease,
> Intent to reason, or polite to please . . .[2]

As befits a conclusion it then develops a more
weighty rhythm.

[1] ii. 261 ff.   [2] iv. 373 ff.

VIII

No poet has confined himself as strictly as Pope did to a confined metre and yet managed so often to astonish the reader with the unpredictable. Some of the examples given above are sufficient to show that Pope's greatest triumph in the couplet lies in his making it dramatic. He can make it sound like actual passionate speech. The Elizabethan dramatists left the couplet for blank verse when they wanted to get similar effects. But Pope's sense of the capacities of the couplet forbade such a transition. And in consequence of his realization of that sense, the reader is excited by the mere distance between these new couplets and Waller's, between the *Imitations of Horace* and *Windsor Forest*. So stately, decorative, courtly a metre is now embodying the accents of normal speech. The complex art is so perfect that it is hidden. The lines read themselves.

> Pretty! in amber to observe the forms
> Of hairs, or straws, or dirt, or grubs, or worms!
> The things, we know, are neither rich nor rare,
> But wonder how the devil they got there.[1]

> Why am I ask'd what next shall see the light?
> Heav'ns! was I born for nothing but to write?[2]

> I lose my patience, and I own it too,
> When works are censur'd, not as bad but new.[3]

> Tho' still some traces of our rustic vein
> And splay-foot verse, remain'd, and will remain.[4]

[1] *Ep. to Arbuthnot*, 169–72.
[2] Id. 271–2.
[3] *Im. of Hor.* Ep. ii. i. To Augustus, 115–16.
[4] Id. 270–1.

> But after all, what would you have me do?
> When out of twenty I can please not two.[1]

> F. Why then so few commended?
>   P. Not so fierce!
> Find you the Virtue, and I'll find the Verse.[2]

> Yes, I am proud; I must be proud to see
> Men not afraid of God, afraid of me.[3]

With these effects goes that of the long word with a single stress. To begin with, Pope used these words for their gravity. Donne had realized the ponderous value of such words: for instance in the famous

> we are swallowed up, irreparably, irrevocably, irrecoverably, irremediably.[4]

In pronouncing words of this kind the reader compensates for the vague pother of weak accents by trebly reinforcing the strong accents. Pope uses them first as Donne did:

> Full in the midst proud Fame's imperial seat,
> With jewels blaz'd, magnificently great.[5]

> . . . the God's Array
> Refulgent, flash'd intolerable Day.[6]

Later Pope came to see the value of these words for producing variously graded effects of contempt:

> With scornful mien, and various toss of air,
> Fantastic, vain, and insolently fair.[7]

> Alive, ridiculous, and dead, forgot![8]

---

[1] *Im. of Hor.* Ep. ii. ii. 80–1.
[2] *Epil. to Sat.* Dial. ii. 104–5.   [3] Id. 208–9.
[4] Sermon LXVI.   [5] *Temple of Fame*, 249–50.
[6] *Iliad*, viii. 53–4. Cf. Dryden, *Knight's Tale*, iii. 81.
[7] *The Looking Glass*, 1–2.
[8] *Mor. Ess.* ii. *Of the Characters of Women*, 248.

It becomes one of the favourite weapons of the *Dunciad*.

> Cibberian forehead, and Cibberian brain.[1]

> Cibberian forehead, or Cimmerian gloom.[2]

> To where Fleet-ditch with disemboguing streams
> Rolls the large tribute of dead dogs to Thames.[3]

> Not so bold Arnall; with a weight of skull,
> Furious he drives, precipitately dull.[4]

> a skull,
> Of solid proof, impenetrably dull.[5]

> A friend in glee, ridiculously grim.[6]

---

[1] *Dunciad*, i. 218.   [2] Id. iv. 532.
[3] Id. ii. 271–2.   [4] Id. 315–16.   [5] Id. iii. 25–6.
[6] Id. 154.

STRATIFICATION AND VARIETY

Pope is unique among English poets in the composite nature of his work. He is seldom doing one thing at a time. In his best work he is doing several things. The epic imitations, the *Moral Essays* and the *Imitations of Horace* show him engineering not one simple effect but a combination of simultaneous effects. There is the versification elaborated into systems of balance or refraining from balance. There is the verbal colouring and effects, such as alliteration, and the use or avoidance of 'poetic diction'. There is the mimicry, the onomatopoeia. There is the invention in the syntax. There is the 'imitation', the warrant in previous literature for the basis of Pope's very meaning. There are the phrasal echoes of older poetry. These effects usually fall in simultaneous combinations of two or more, and it is principally because of this that Pope achieves his peculiar intensity. Pope writes on the assumption that his reader finds it exciting to discover layer below layer. He writes on the assumption that the reader is intelligent as well as sensitive, that he does not shrink from working if work provides him with wages.

I

The best instance of the quality of the verbal colouring on a large scale is the *Dunciad* in which Pope is almost continuously working an alliteration of *b, d, f, m, k, g,* and *l.* The first three of these letters

are associated with swearing and indecency and this
not accidentally but because of their capacity for
brutal emphasis. (One recalls Macbeth's

> The devil damn thee black, thou cream-faced loon,

Fuller's instance of William Perkins, 'The Learned,
pious and painfull Preacher', who pronounced *damn*
with such awful weight,[1] or Atterbury's line on Lord
Cadogan:

> A bold, bad, blundering, blustering, bloody booby.[2])

In smaller ways Pope uses alliteration and assonance
to sharpen his contrasts:

> Die, and endow a College, or a Cat.[3]
>
> A Fop their Passion, but their Prize a Sot.[4]
>
> Slow rose a form, in majesty of Mud.[5]

In the first instance the reader having encountered
the two spaced *d*s expects the first *c* of the second half
of the line to be followed by a second. But being
schooled in Pope's effects he expects a contrast as
well as an agreement. *Cat*, when it comes, produces
therefore two simultaneous effects. There are often
these verbal qualities emphasizing, coinciding with,
the qualities of the versification.

II

With these effects may be grouped those in which
Pope mimics other qualities in his meaning. In the

[1] 'He would pronounce the word *Damne* with such an emphasis, as
left a dolefull Echo in his auditours ears a good while after'. *Holy and
Profane State* (1642), pp. 88 and 90.   [2] Spence, 156.
[3] *Mor. Ess.* III. *Of the Use of Riches*. To Bathurst, 96.
[4] *Mor. Ess.* II. *Of the Characters of Women*, 247.
[5] *Dunciad*, ii. 326.

lines on Dryden quoted above he reproduces Dryden's style. The line condemning expletives in the *Essay on Criticism*—

> While expletives their feeble aid do join[1]

—contains an example of one in the act of joining its feeble aid. The dullness of monosyllabic lines is stated and illustrated simultaneously:

> And ten low words oft creep in one dull line.[2]

The unending decorations of seventeenth-century verse, in which a little stuff has to go a long way, have their length mimicked in the length of the line in time and type:

> One Simile, that solitary shines
> In the dry desert of a thousand lines,
> Or lengthen'd Thought that gleams through many a page,
> Has sanctify'd whole poems for an age.[3]

In the *Dunciad* antiquarian scholars are mocked in a 'no language' intended to suggest the materials of their study:

> But who is he, in closet close y-pent,
> Of sober face, with learned dust-besprent?
> Right well mine eyes arede the myster wight,
> On parchment scraps y-fed, and Wormius hight.
> To future ages may thy dulness last,
> As thou preserv'st the dulness of the past![4]

---

[1] 346.   [2] Id. 347.

[3] *Im. of Hor.* Ep. ii. i. To Augustus, 111 ff. Cf. the 'Amplifiers' of the *Peri Bathous,* 'who can extend half a dozen thin Thoughts over a whole Folio' (Chap. viii).

[4] iii. 185 ff.

III

The 'imitation' of Chaucer, or Horace, or the epic poem adds another layer to the complexity. It was a belief in contemporary criticism that

over and above a just Painting of Nature, a learned Reader will find a new Beauty superadded in a happy Imitation of some famous Ancient, as it revives in his Mind the Pleasure he took in first reading such an Author.[1]

Pope first took to imitating, he told Spence,

not out of vanity, but humility: I saw how defective my own things were; and endeavoured to mend my manner, by copying good strokes from others.[2]

He continued imitating, not out of humility, but because he found that the particular composite effects he was aiming at benefited from this increased area of sensitiveness which he was requiring in the mind of his reader. The reader has continually to be thinking of the parallel in Chaucer, Donne, Horace, or the epic poem, noting resemblance and difference. For instance, the after-world of the sylphs contains the kind of spirit for whom

> Her joy in gilded Chariots, when alive,
> And love of Ombre, after death survive.[3]

These lines are almost a quotation from Dryden's *Aeneid*:

> The love of Horses which they had, alive,
> And care of Chariots, after Death survive.[4]

[1] *Guardian*, No. 12. See the whole passage.
[2] 278.   [3] *Rape of the Lock*, i. 55–6.
[4] vi. 890–1.

which translated

> . . . quae gratia currum
> Armorumque fuit vivis, quae cura nitentes
> Pascere equos, eadem sequitur tellure repostos.[1]

In this passage *ombre* provides a difference, *chariots* a sameness. But, looking at *chariots* again, the reader perceives a difference lying beyond this sameness: the chariot of the epic heroes was by no means the same thing as what was called chariot in 1714— the gilded carriage with its six Flanders mares. In the adaptation of the first ode of Horace's fourth Book, the meaning and tone of Pope's

> I am not now, alas! the man
>   As in the gentle Reign of My Queen Anne,

depend upon the reader's realization that in the original

> Non sum qualis eram bonae
>   Sub regno Cinarae

Cinara was a mistress. It is the same on a larger scale in the parody of the epic form. Everything in the *Rape of the Lock* seems to be there in its own right. But in point of fact nothing is there which is not warranted by something or other in epic poetry before Pope. Belinda's petticoat is perfectly indicated: the quality of the description may be tested, for example, by the trembling expansiveness of the last line—

> To fifty chosen Sylphs, of special note,
> We trust th'important charge, the Petticoat:
> Oft have we known that sevenfold fence to fail,
> Tho' stiff with hoops, and arm'd with ribs of whale;

[1] vi. 653-5.

> Form a strong line about the silver bound,
> And guard the wide circumference around.[1]

Belinda's petticoat, again, is part of the feminine satire of the poem: 'Oft have we known . . .' But it is in the poem also because it is Pope's counterpart to the shields of epic heroes: and Vulcan, making Achilles' shield in the eighteenth Book of the *Iliad*, binds its circumference with silver. In the same way the nodding heads of the 'three College Sophs' and the 'three pert Templars' reading bad poetry are compared to pines in a simile perfect in its 'beauty':

> As to soft gales top-heavy pines bow low
> Their heads, and lift them as they cease to blow.[2]

But the simile is there, not simply or primarily for its beauty, but because Statius had used a cypress bowing and lifting in the south wind as a simile for heroes wrestling,[3] and Lucan had used a forest of pines in a similar fashion to describe the loudness of the shouts of heroes,[4] both similes making Pope's scholars look ridiculous by the towering discrepancy. On the authority of Le Bossu, a critic whom Pope deeply respected, the epic poem was based on a moral. Pope based the *Rape of the Lock* firmly on an admirable moral, but when in the 1717 edition he inserted Clarissa's speech 'to open more clearly the Moral of the Poem', he enunciated it in the form of an almost word-for-word adaptation of his own

---

[1] ii. 117 ff.
[2] *Dunciad*, ii. 391-2.
[3] *Thebaid*, vi. 854-7.
[4] *Civil War*, i. 388-91.

translation of Sarpedon's speech to Glaucus from
Iliad XII. Pope is out to make his poem perfect
from whatever angle it is seen, to 'surprise' the reader
by a 'fine' and accurate 'excess' of interest. If he
is imitating the epic form he will see that the imitation
is not only as elaborate as possible but complete
and accurate from all points of view. The epic poem,
for example, is not complete without battles.
Boileau's *Lutrin* had mimicked a Homeric battle by
means of books, Garth's *Dispensary* by means of
gallipots, urinals and brass-weights. Pope has his
battle with fans and snuff. But he provides a parody
twice intensified by having also a battle in the form
of a game of ombre. He arranges it so that this
game-battle is the most exciting possible. Yet every
step in its suspense had to be in accord with the
complicated laws of the game. Far more than any
other poet Pope would have seen a precise meaning
in Rossetti's phrase 'the fundamental brain work of
poetry'. There are few poets who would turn away
from their poem to try out various games of ombre
and then turn back again and versify the one that
most perfectly fitted their purpose. This presence
of brain-work in such quantity and quality cannot be
said to rob the poem of any of its emotional value
even for a reader whose nineteenth-century sym-
pathies incline him to think that poetry is a divine
afflatus dependent on the brain only so far as to
divide it from madness. There are elements in
Pope's poetry which adequately provide for this
kind of reader. But for other readers all these
accurate mechanics of the brain are themselves found

to contribute to the emotional value of the poem.
The gnomes are directing,

> to every atom just,
> The pungent grains of titillating dust.

IV

The idiosyncrasies of language, the syntax, are laid
under contribution. It is part of Pope's realization
that what are often ornaments can for him be factors
in the sharpening of his points. He seeks out words
which can bear double meanings both of which are
valuable for his purpose. In the *Essay of Criticism*
part of the description of Restoration letters reads:

> Pulpits their sacred satire learn'd to spare,
> And Vice admir'd to find a flatt'rer there!
> Encourag'd thus, Wit's Titans brav'd the skies,
> And the press groan'd with licens'd blasphemies.[1]

'Brav'd' here has the two meanings noted by Johnson
in his Dictionary: (*a*) 'to carry a boasting appearance',
and (*b*) 'to defy'. 'Skies' supplements the obvious
meaning with that of 'heaven', and so bears out both
meanings of 'brav'd'. Similarly 'licens'd' means that
the blasphemies bore the official *imprimatur* despite
their being 'licentious'. (Johnson remembered this
pun and reproduced it.)[2] The press 'groan'd' because it was both overworked and ashamed of its
master.

Again, in the cave of Spleen Umbriel discovers what
at first sight looks like a typical allegorical group:
the goddess

[1] 550 ff.   [2] *London,* 59.

> . . . sighs for ever on her pensive bed,
> Pain at her side, and Megrim at her head.[1]

But contemporary readers well knew that the pain of spleen was felt in the side, that of megrim in the head. *At her side* and *at her head* have both two meanings, internal and external, both of which Pope is using.[2] It is the same in the *Dunciad*:

> Int'rest that waves on Party-colour'd wings[3]

or

> O! pass more innocent, in infant state,
> To the mild Limbo of our Father Tate:
> Or peaceably forgot, at once be blest
> In Shadwell's bosom with eternal Rest![4]

'Father' means progenitor and also carries a reference to Father Abraham, which 'bosom' develops.

Spectator No. 61 had discountenanced the pun, and Pope in the *Peri Bathous* is found mocking at it. Chapter X of that work begins the discussion of Tropes and Figures, and a subdivision, *The Mixture of Figures*, includes as its third item *The Paranomasia, or Pun*,

> where a Word, like the tongue of a jackdaw, speaks twice as much by being split: As this of Mr. Dennis,
>
> > *Bullets that wound, like Parthians, as they* fly;
> > > [*Poems*, 1693, p. 13]
>
> or this excellent one of Mr. Welsted,
>
> > *Behold the Virgin lye*
> > *Naked, and only* cover'd *by the* Sky.
> > > [*Acon and Lavinia*]

Pope's impatience with Shakespeare's puns was

---

[1] *Rape of the Lock*, iv. 23–4.
[2] See Mr. Lawrence Babb's article on the Cave of Spleen, *Review of English Studies*, April 1936, 165 ff.   [3] iv. 538.   [4] i. 237 ff.

versified for him by David Mallet in a poem dedicated
to Pope:

> Sad Hamlet quibbles, and the hearer sleeps.[1]

Pope himself made puns in his poems but with this
distinction, that he kept them in what he considered
their proper place, unlike Addison who would have
banished them completely. What annoyed him in
Dennis, Welsted, and Shakespeare was the use of a
comic figure at serious moments and for serious
purposes. He disliked puns at serious moments as
he disliked metaphysical wit in serious love-poems.
It was because Hamlet was sad that his quibbles
were disgusting. To make sad Hamlet or the dying
Gaunt play with language was an offence against
Nature, since, despite Romeo's observation,[2] most
men were serious at such moments. Horace had
laid it down that sad words became a face of sorrow
and jests a merry one.[3] The *Rape of the Lock*, the
Dunciad, the Essays and Epistles found an appropriate use for puns. But there are no puns in *Eloisa
to Abelard*.

V

Pope's syntax is always as compressed as possible.
His meaning is left to grow at leisure out of its confined context. One of his chief methods is the
conjunction, the monosyllabic 'low' word which
lays together in apparently tame accord the strangest
of bedfellows:

> Who give th'hysteric, or poetic fit.[4]

[1] *Of Verbal Criticism. To Mr. Pope*, 58. Cf. *Spectator*, No. 61.
[2] v. iii. 88 ff.   [3] *Ars Poetica*, 99 ff.
[4] *Rape of the Lock*, iv. 60.

To rest, the Cushion and soft Dean invite.[1]

Wrapt in a gown, for sickness, and for show.[2]

Proud as a Peeress, prouder as a Punk.[3]

A Fop their Passion, but their Prize a Sot.[4]

The first instance is taken from Umbriel's address to the Goddess Spleen, and the worth of the line lies in the ambiguities started by the *or*. This *or* may represent an *alias*, an absolute, another word for the same thing. This reading would mean that hysteria is poetry, poetry hysteria. On the other hand, the *or* may represent a choice between the two things, which would mean that it is a toss-up whether a lady becomes hysterical or poetic, that, though they are very different things, she is not the person to know it. The doubleness of these different meanings is discovered by the reader's analysis of two possible syntactical relationships.

In the last quotation the most potent word is *but*. A *but* introduces a contrast, usually a complete one. Here the change is not from bad to good but from a fop to a sot, from one kind of bad to another. (The let-down is the more severe because of the confidence-trick played by the splendid strut of the inversion.) Pope expresses his concise meaning as much through points of syntax as through vocabulary.[5]

[1] *Mor. Ess.* iv. *Of the Use of Riches.* To Burlington. 149.
[2] *Rape of the Lock*, iv. 36.
[3] *Mor. Ess.* II. *Of the Characters of Women.* 70.
[4] Id. 247.
[5] Mr. Empson in his *Seven Types of Ambiguity* (1930) makes some excellent analyses of certain passages from Pope. He is undecided as to how far the 'ambiguities [of eighteenth-century poets] are typical of

VI

Among English poets Pope is one of the most greedy of other poets' phrases. It was all part of his aim to make the reader work, to keep him from sleep —the opiate quality of bad poetry was his constant butt. The reader is made to take pleasure in the quality and extent of his reading. At the lowest estimate, there is this pleasure. But there is more besides. Sometimes one has the pleasure of recognizing that a compliment is being paid. For example, in the line

Die of a rose in aromatic pain[1]

the last two words are a quotation from the Countess of Winchelsea's *Spleen*.[2] Pope is quoting here in the same way that, when he was using any word, he was, so to speak, consciously taking it from the dictionary. He considered *aromatic pain* an addition to the language, its two words having almost the value of a recognized common noun. But often Pope gives

their age and method' and 'how fundamental for understanding their verse' (p. 87). Ambiguities, as my present chapter shows, were fundamental in Pope's method and were more specifically ambiguities of syntax and 'imitation' than Mr. Empson perhaps realizes. Some of his analyses of Pope (like others in his book) suffer from being based on a faulty transcription of the words under analysis. This is particularly unfortunate at p. 189 where Pope is made to write:

A fop her passion, and her prize a sot.

In other instances, Mr. Empson's occasionally defective historical sense makes ambiguities which did not exist for Pope, and misses others which did exist for him. But one is grateful indeed for the three pages (91-4) devoted to Clarissa's speech in the *Rape of the Lock* (though here the 'thoughtless mortals' should be 'dejected' not 'digested').

[1] *Ess. on Man*, i. 200.

[2] Lytton Strachey was unfortunate in singling out this phrase as his example of Pope's 'sensuously beautiful' quality (See *Pope* (1925) 27). His point does not, of course, suffer by this mistake.

the reader the finer pleasure of seeing a tame or good thing in another poet lifted and made far more incisive. He provides a phrase with its culmination. As an example of this one might take the line:

> And Alma Mater lie dissolv'd in port![1]

This expression derives in the first place from Ovid. Line 612 of Book XI of the *Metamorphoses* reads:

> Quo cubat ipse deus membris languore solutis.

Sandys translates by

> Here lay the lazie God, dissolu'd in rest.

When Dryden came to the same line in his translation he avoided the literal perfection of Sandys's line and wrote:

> . . . where lay the God
> And slept supine, his Limbs display'd abroad.

But he remembered the phrase when translating the story of Cymon and Iphigenia from Boccaccio, and at line 550 spoke of

> . . . Men dissolv'd in ease.

In Ozell's translation of *Le Lutrin* (1708), 'dissolv'd in ease' appears twice and once again as 'dissolv'd in thoughtless ease'. In Rowe's translation of Lucan's *Civil War*,

> emollit gentes clementia coeli[2]

becomes

> . . . *Asia*'s softer Climate, form'd to please,
> Dissolves her Sons in Indolence and Ease.[3]

So far, in all these poets, the phrase has remained virtually static. Pope provides it with its culmina-

---

[1] *Dunciad,* iii. 338.   [2] viii. 366.   [3] viii. 485–6.

tion. His line requires the co-operation of the reader's memory. After 'dissolv'd in' the reader expects 'ease' but gets 'port'. But the complication does not stop there. 'Port' has a reflexive action on 'dissolv'd in'. The reader has already been at pleasant pains to recognize this verb as figurative. He must now return and allow it its literal meaning since port, unlike rest and ease, is a liquid and therefore a solvent. But the figurative sense persists since the traditional phrases, dissolv'd-in-rest and -ease, equally apply to the dons of the eighteenth century. This mixture of abstract and concrete in 'dissolv'd in' produces a slightly dazed perplexity in the reader, but not until the words have been read a second time. Pope, that is, first requires the reader to work— recognizing (the beginning of) a traditional phrase, linking dons with Morpheus who was the subject of the verb in Ovid and Sandys. He then requires him to start working again, partly undoing his former labour. A line already accepted as complex has to be reaccepted as still more complex and complex in different ways. Pope found in other poets' phrases a convenient machinery for producing this kind of effect, for making a line not simply a path between two points but a maze—a maze with a sure clue.

As another instance one might take the lines describing Curll's performance in the poetic games. He has fallen in the mire but is unashamed: he

> scours and stinks along;
> Re-passes Lintot, vindicates the race
> Nor heeds the brown dishonours of his face.[1]

[1] *Dunciad*, ii. 106 ff.

'Brown' was a word which Dante had applied to the air of evening,[1] which Milton had used on several occasions to describe shade, and Dryden to describe horror in woods. This connotation had become standard. Pope himself had 'breathe[d] a browner horror on the woods' in *Eloisa to Abelard*.[2] Pope for Curll's annoyance takes a fashionable word, strips it of its literary connotation and reverts to its plain sense. That plain sense as applied to Curll is only too plain. There might be doubt about the brownness of horror in woods but there could be none about that on Curll's face. In the same line, again, there is the phrase 'dishonours of his face'. 'The honours of his head' was a fairly common phrase in the translations of epic, and in other dignified poems, for the locks of Jove or heroes or for the boughs or leaves of trees.[3] Both Dryden and Pope had already used the phrase for epic parody: in *Mac Flecknoe* (134) and in the *Rape of the Lock* (iv. 135 and 140). So that when Pope further improves it by the addition of a negative prefix, he is rubbing in the extent of Curll's lamentable unlikeness to the god and heroes of the epics, to great trees, and even to Belinda and the wretched Flecknoe. He intends the phrase to have also its ordinary meaning—the addition of 'dis-' and the substitution of 'face' for 'head' shock the reader into allowing the phrase its surface value as well as its value for parody. This kind of imitation

---

[1] *Inferno*, ii. 1.   [2] 170.
[3] See, for example, Dryden's *Æneid*, x. 172, Pope's *Iliad*, xv. 45, his *Odyssey*, xi. 235 and xviii. 182, the *Pastorals* (*Winter*, 32) and *Windsor Forest*, 221.

was as important for Pope's verse as any other
element.

VII

It is because of all this composite activity that the
cruelty of Pope's wit and the indecency of some of
his material and of his innuendos are deflected from
mere offensiveness. The cruelty and indecency are
elements in the chiaroscuro, mixed up with the
element of a fine yet almost tropical beauty, so that
it is impossible to tell where one ends and the other
begins. One might as readily attempt to distinguish
beauty and filth in the unified worlds of *Troilus and
Cressida* or *Measure for Measure*, of the *Way of the
World* or in life itself. In the character of Sporus
the reader's mind is kept so busy merely taking in
the baroque zigzag of beauty and nastiness that
Hervey is forgotten. Words like 'Beauty that
shocks you' provide too much to think about, en-
large the mind too excitingly for it to centre itself in
narrow superciliousness on a weak human character.
It is the same in the *Dunciad*. The laughter at
Cibber, at Curll and the rest occupies a mere corner
in the universal illumination of the ludicrous and the
sordid. And, to some extent, it must have been so
at the date of the first publication. Spence records
an interesting remark of Lockier, Dean of Peter-
borough:

Pope's character of Addison is one of the truest, as well as
one of the best things he ever wrote: Addison deserved that
character the most of any man.[1]

[1] 57.

It is possible to read this as meaning that Atticus is not Addison, but that Addison comes nearest to being Atticus. The character of Atticus (unlike a character in *Absalom and Achitophel*) is too intense to apply merely to Addison or any human being. While one reads one is watching Pope in the repeated acts of materializing a sly, mean hypocrisy which is so intense that it transfigures its immediate object and creates the genius of that vice. The character of Atticus belongs to the small group of sublime 'humours' to which Volpone and Tartuffe belong. And because of the very perfection of the surface of the poem, it is possible to read the *Rape of the Lock*, and even much of the *Dunciad*, without realizing that below the exquisite scintillation an ingenious obscenity is sometimes curling and uncurling itself. Where, one may ask, is the line to divide Virgilian tenderness from sexual suggestion in the last couplet of the 4th Canto of the *Rape of the Lock*? And one has only to compare the passage ending

> Sign'd with that Ichor which from Gods distils.[1]

with the passage from its source, Ozell's translation of Tassoni's *Secchia Rapita*, to see what gulfs separate Pope's brilliant amalgam of elements contradictory yet complementary from the bare indecency of Ozell.[2] In Pope indeed the beauty seems more

---

[1] *Dunciad,* ii. 83–92.

[2] The Thieving God came next; his Right Hand bore
  The Spectacles and Hat of *Jupiter*;
  And in his Left a huge green Bag he held,
  With *Mortals* Cases and Addresses fill'd:

powerful than the indecency. Pope is again multi-
plying his vertical effects. In a similar way, when
the literal theme is faded wrinkled society women,
the effect of what one can only describe as a melancholy Virgilian tenderness melts away the Hogarthian
grotesqueness:

> Asham'd to own they gave delight before,
> Reduc'd to feign it, when they give no more:
> As Hags hold Sabbaths, less for joy than spite,
> So these their merry, miserable Night;
> Still round and round the Ghosts of Beauty glide,
> And haunt the places where their Honour died.[1]

VIII

All this is what one might call the vertical variety
of Pope's verse. A horizontal variety is equally
remarkable. Variety was recognized by the eighteenth century generally as a valuable factor in an
aesthetic effect. *Variety* and *various* are favourite
words. 'Not', as Dr. Richards notes, 'that there is
any virtue in variety by itself, . . . a page of the
dictionary can show more variety than any page of
poetry.'[2] Variety has value when a poem, unlike the
dictionary, connects all the various elements together.
Dr. Johnson commends variety wherever he meets it.

> These afterwards, in solemn Form, he plac'd
> On two Close-Stools which *Jove*'s Back-Closet grac'd;
> There, twice a Day, Mankind's Requests are sure
> To be perus'd, and pass the *Signature*.
>
> (*La Secchia Rapita: The Trophy-Bucket* (1713) D 2ʳ).

'Addresses' is the MS. correction for 'Petitions' in the B.M. copy,
1063. g. 26. It probably had Ozell's authority.

[1] *Mor. Ess.* ii, *On the Characters of Women*, 237 ff.
[2] *Principles of Criticism* (1925) 240.

Pope is the most connectedly various of poets. A poem of his usually offers several effects simultaneously but it seldom allows them to be prolonged. A few lines later in the poem and the whole topography has changed. This is an additional reason why Pope must be read slowly enough for intentness. The materials are concentrated and must be allowed to 'open' themselves—to use a favourite word of Pope's. Otherwise the poem may seem a series of small inadequate patches.

CONCLUSION

THE problem for the critic of Pope's poetry is that of relating the mechanics of the verse to its quality for the emotions. This emotional quality is felt by many readers, though not by all. Often the failure to experience it is due to unfamiliarity with Pope's poetry, persistence in thinking of him as a poet of *sententiae*. Pope's fame as a gnomic writer has often proved a barrier to his fame as a poetical poet. It has attracted the wrong readers and kept away the right ones. Pope did not proclaim as his favourite line:

> A *little learning* is a dang'rous thing.[1]

The couplet he did single out was one which most pleased his ear, the one indeed which Keats might have chosen for him:

> Lo! where Mæotis sleeps, and hardly flows
> The freezing Tanais thro' a waste of snows.[2]

Pope states that he chose verse as the medium for the *Essay on Man* for reasons which he enumerates, but he knew that the material was, apart from those reasons, mainly material for prose. He should not be judged by his *Essay on Man* or the *Essay on Criticism*, though even in these works the poetry has been underrated. Nor must he be judged by his *Pastorals* and *Windsor Forest*, unless the judge will

---

[1] *Ess. on Crit.* 215.
[2] See Johnson's *Lives*, ed. G. Birkbeck Hill, iii. 250.

qualify his sentence by understanding into what context of historical principles these poems fall. Nor must he be judged on the *Rape of the Lock* unless the judge, before he begins to judge, will understand that because a poem is about the work of a pair of scissors on a lock of hair it is not therefore necessarily a trivial poem. (We have heard too much about the 'delicate filigree' of that poem.[1]) Nor must Pope be judged by his 'pathetic' pieces —that is, the pieces more directly addressed to the emotions—unless the judge understands that his method of writing in these poems is often one of hiding emotion away, of saying indirectly what he felt. Pope set himself against the Elizabethan methods of writing passionate poetry, which in turn became those of the nineteenth century. He did not go directly to work by crying out with Shakespeare

[1] Pope is too often thought of as an expert in miniature (see, for example, T. S. Eliot's essay on Dryden). His expertness in miniature is usually combined with expertness on the grand scale. Even in a poem like the *Rape of the Lock*, where the excellence mainly depends on the mimicry of heroic things by exquisite, there are passages of largeness and power: for example

    And calls forth all the wonders of her face (i. 142)

    And the pale ghosts start at the flash of day! (v. 52)

And what is there miniature about the *Dunciad*? All Pope's satires indeed are life-size. Even in the *Rape of the Lock* the politicians are not pigmies:

    Coffee, (which makes the politician wise,

    And see thro' all things with his half-shut eyes) (iii. 117–8)

and Timon is

    A puny insect, shiv'ring at a breeze!

(*Mor. Essays*, iv. *Of the Use of Riches*. To Burlington, 108) simply because he has dwarfed himself by the preposterous enormity of his façade.

Pope may be said to excel all English poets in his combination of size with minuteness. It is part of the variety he sought for.

(in the sonnets) or Donne that his heart was feeling this and that grief or rapture. When, at the close of *Eloisa to Abelard*, Pope tells a woman—it is probably Lady Mary Wortley Montagu—that he loves her, he says it by means of a picture of other lovers; and, moreover, by means of other lovers whom Eloisa imagines as hoping that they will never love as she and Abelard loved—the twofold indirection of Eloisa's vision of two other lovers made threefold by a negative. His profoundest love-poem is given the form of an imitation of one of Horace's odes. He may speak his less passionate emotion directly, but it is controlled before he begins. We know from a hundred independent sources that Pope had the true fire in him, but he did not set it before the reader's eyes as a bare flame. He set it instead to turn

> . . . ev'ry wheel of that unweary'd Mill
> That turn'd ten thousand verses . . .[1]

Pope was under no delusions about the nature of the reader's response to poetry. If dramatic poetry, for instance, did not affect the emotions it was merely verse:

> Yet lest you think I rally more than teach,
> Or praise malignly Arts I cannot reach,
> Let me for once presume t'instruct the times,
> To know the Poet from the Man of rhymes:
> 'Tis he, who gives my breast a thousand pains,
> Can make me feel each Passion that he feigns;
> Enrage, compose, with more than magic Art,
> With Pity, and with Terror, tear my heart . . .[2]

[1] *Im. of Hor.* Ep. II. ii, 77 f.
[2] Ibid., i. To Augustus. 338 ff.

Even satire must touch the 'Passions':

To attack Vices in the abstract, without touching Persons, may be safe fighting indeed, but it is fighting with Shadows. General propositions are obscure, misty, and uncertain, compar'd with plain, full and home examples: Precepts only apply to our Reason, which in most men is but weak: Examples are pictures, and strike the Senses, nay raise the Passions, and call in those (the strongest and most general of all motives) to the aid of reformation. . . .[1]

Pope's methods of touching the reader's passions, of arousing his emotional response, were mainly those of clear statement,

Something in Verse as true as Prose,[2]

poetry, as Crabbe put it, without an atmosphere.[3] He had no use for poetry or prose which aroused the emotions only at the expense of divorcing them from intelligence, reason and Nature, and leading them off in a round of bedazzlement and inebriety. And he disliked equally the poetry of some of Donne's followers in which the intelligence is so much teased that the emotions are left unaffected. Yet he partly resembled the metaphysicals, since he was out to offer something of value to the understanding.[4] To make his kind of poetry he relied partly on the intellectual quality of what he was saying. And his poetry serves to demonstrate the proximity, the

[1] Letter to Arbuthnot, 26 July 1734.

[2] Swift's part of the imitation of Horace's *Satires* II. vi, which Pope completed, l. 26.

[3] *Life and Poems of . . . Crabbe* (1834), iv. 144.

[4] See F. R. Leavis, *Revaluation* (1936), 70 ff. for a statement of the metaphysical 'wit' in Pope. This element seems to have been first noted by J. Middleton Murry (*Countries of the Mind*, ed. 1931, 60).

interpenetrableness, of the intellect and the emotions. La Rochefoucauld, writing in prose, affects one's emotions though he is only concerned with one's intellect. I take La Rochefoucauld because his maxims provide very nearly the same intellectual interest as one of the best kinds of Pope's poetry. But La Rochefoucauld is only an extreme example of what all the best prose provides. It addresses itself to the intellect yet the emotions are magnetized into its electric circle. But Pope would have been the first to acknowledge that the maxims of La Rochefoucauld and those similar passages in his own prose were not poetry. Before such material became poetry, it required to be radically changed. One can see what this transformation amounted to if one compares the passage on Addison's character in Pope's prose letter to Craggs (dated 15 July 1715) with the character as it appears in the verse *Epistle to Arbuthnot*. The prose character runs:

We have, it seems, a great Turk in poetry, who can never bear a brother on the throne; and has his mutes too, a sett of nodders, winkers, and whisperers, whose business is to strangle all other offsprings of wit in their birth. The new translator of Homer [Tickell] is the humblest slave he has, that is to say, his first Minister; let him receive the honours he gives me, but receive them with fear and trembling; let him be proud of the approbation of his absolute Lord. . . . But after all I have said of this great man, there is no rupture between us. We are each of us so civil and obliging, that neither thinks he is obliged: And I, for my part, treat with him, as we do with the Grand Monarch; who has too many great qualities not to be respected, though we know he watches any occasion to oppress us.

In the *Epistle to Arbuthnot* this appears as:

> Peace to all such! but were there One whose fires
> True Genius kindles, and fair Fame inspires;
> Blest with each talent and each art to please,
> And born to write, converse, and live with ease:
> Should such a man, too fond to rule alone,
> Bear, like the Turk, no brother near the throne,
> View him with scornful, yet with jealous eyes,
> And hate for arts that caus'd himself to rise;
> Damn with faint praise, assent with civil leer,
> And without sneering, teach the rest to sneer;
> Willing to wound, and yet afraid to strike,
> Just hint a fault, and hesitate dislike;
> Alike reserv'd to blame, or to commend,
> A tim'rous foe, and a suspicious friend;
> Dreading ev'n fools, by Flatterers besieg'd,
> And so obliging, that he ne'er oblig'd;
> Like *Cato*, give his little Senate laws,
> And sit attentive to his own applause;
> While Wits and Templars ev'ry sentence raise,
> And wonder with a foolish face of praise:—
> Who but must laugh, if such a man there be?
> Who would not weep, if ATTICUS were he?[1]

The transformation here is radical. There are, first of all, the external marks which distinguish all good verse from prose. The verse is more concise. (In *The Design* before the *Essay on Man* Pope noted that verse expressed things 'more *shortly*' than prose.) Its words are more intense and their quality as words attracts more attention—this distinction of Coleridge's between the words of poetry and prose would have had Pope's support. And there is what

[1] 193 ff.

one can inadequately call the rhythm of the couplets. But, as reason for these differences, there is a lyrical impulse behind the verse. This impulse is observable in the stated meaning:

> Peace to all such! But were there one . . .

and

> Who but must laugh . . .
> Who would not weep . . .?

But it need not be so observable. The lyrical impulse is equally there behind the character of Sporus in the same *Epistle* and equally absent from the consummate prose *Letter to a Noble Lord*. Pope's attempts at lyric measures are, when seriously 'beautiful', usually of second-rate value. His genius did not move lightly enough in the song. His proper measures are slower, longer, more grave. But this does not mean that his impulses were any the less lyrical at their source. They moved his 'heart' as deeply though they moved it to something nearer melancholy than elation. In this he was like his favourite Virgil in whom the tears of things ache and burn behind the solid epic. And it is this quality which constitutes part of his profound kinship with Mozart and Keats.

This mood was both fed and communicated by the act of composition. The methods of the verse developed it, while they expressed it, complicating it in a dozen ways. Most of the poetry of Pope demanded verse from the start, that is, the emotions which engendered it were strongly enough involved and were the kind of emotions which only metre could set at rest. But since any long poem cannot equally be the same kind of poetry from the moment of its first stirring onwards, there is inevitably an admixture of material in Pope's longer poems which had to be given its poetry. Pope improved such material till it could stand the strain of being given its poetry. Or he arranged it so exquisitely on paper that the reader's emotions, though slackened, were not let down. This is when things are at their lowest, but at their highest La Rochefoucauld, iambs, imitations, Sporus, are forgotten. One's emotions rage like tigers round the intellectual circle and rage all the more powerfully for the complexity of Pope's methods. In the 'pathetic' poetry, the machinery of reticence has an opposite effect. The circle is now a solid barrier receiving the impact of the poet's emotions and preserving them from dissipation in panic and madness, or in the pain of silence. The complex perfection of the metre provides the reader with a sense of passionate melancholy controlled with difficulty. The stricken poet is master.

Pope, therefore, 'pleases' by his 'sentiment'. In the *Advertisement* before the *Epistle to Arbuthnot* he bracketed 'sentiment' with 'truth' as the two things he had aimed at:

If [the Epistle] have any thing pleasing, it will be that by which I am most desirous to please, the *Truth* and the *Sentiment*.

By truth Pope meant fact, the actualities of the life around him. And, at times, satire seemed to him no more than a record of those actualities. There were

times when he wearied of Bufo, of Timon, of Atticus,
feeling confined to the plain when heights were
within his reach. A moment of such restlessness is
preserved in a letter to Swift of 19 December 1734,
written when the long, piecemeal labour on the
Epistle to Arbuthnot was nearing publication. Its
statement can therefore be set against the sentence
from the *Advertisement*. Pope is envying Swift the
freedom of invention allowed by such a work as
Gulliver's Travels. His own essays and epistles
allowed him no such wings:

My system is a short one, and my circle narrow. Imagination has no limits, and that is a sphere in which you may
move on to eternity; but where one is confined to truth, or,
to speak more like a human creature, to the appearances of
truth, we soon find the shortness of our tether.

In his unwritten wild 'Persian' fable, Pope had
considered an escape like that of Swift. Later he
considered one of another kind: he planned and even
began his epic *Brutus*. Perhaps Wordsworth would
have hailed *Brutus* as an escape bound for the
'heights'—a blank verse epic would surely have
brought Pope nearer to Thomson, Dyer and even
to Collins, the poets with whom Wordsworth con-
trasted him. But the 'sphere' of 'imagination' which
Pope saw Swift moving in was not that of these
poets. In his letter to Swift 'imagination' meant
something like 'fancy'. Thomson, Dyer (in his
Ruins of Rome), and Collins were 'imaginative' in a
more Coleridgean sense than this. But Pope escaped
his 'system' of 'truth' as certainly as they, and not
by way of fancy. He escaped from it as Wordsworth

escaped from it in the *Prelude*. He interpreted the
human material of his essays and satires as pro-
foundly and nobly as Wordsworth, though not as
'mystically'. Like Wordsworth he transfigured it
with his 'sentiment'. And, more than was necessary
for Wordsworth, he created out of it an unexpected,
even at times an irrelevant beauty—such was his
exaltation. In the *Dunciad* there was all the free
invention of Swift, and, besides this, the burning
laughter, the grandeur, colours, and militant beauty.
And, in this poem and the rest, there was the verse.
Pope's verse is, of course, almost faultless. Its faultlessness indeed has sometimes been made a reproach.
Byron denounced this heresy,[1] and his anger was just
since Pope's faultlessness is not of a kind to detract
from his quality as a poetical poet. It is not a trick,
a mere skill of the brain. Even the lawyer Sir
William Blackstone saw Pope's 'lyre' as 'heav'n-
strung'.[2] Perfection at the pitch attained by Pope
is itself mysterious. The 'heights' were within
Pope's reach and he reached them.

[1] *Works. Letters and Journals*, ed. R. E. Prothero (1898 ff.), v. 506.
[2] *The Lawyer's Farewell to his Muse. Written in the Year 1744.*
(Dodsley's *Collection of Poems*, ed. 1770, iv. 226.)

NOTE ON POPE'S DESCRIPTION

ONE of the most characteristic things about Pope is that the Keats-like quality of his senses is often most apparent when he is bristling with annoyance. Pope's most sensuous descriptive poetry is seldom independent of physical irritation. It is the *suffering* eye[1] which stings Pope into his most elaborate luxuriance of vision. The description of the sylphs in the *Rape of the Lock* is obviously as finely conceived as any of the fairy poetry of Shakespeare, Browne, Herrick, Milton or Dryden. But it is the lines in which Ariel threatens the sylphs with tortures that fire, light, and fill the imagination of the reader:

> Whatever spirit, careless of his charge,
> His post neglects, or leaves the fair at large,
> Shall feel sharp vengeance soon o'ertake his sins,
> Be stopp'd in vials, or transfix'd with pins;
> Or plung'd in lakes of bitter washes lie,
> Or wedg'd whole ages in a bodkin's eye:
> Gums and Pomatums shall his flight restrain,
> While clogg'd he beats his silken wings in vain;
> Or Alum styptics with contracting pow'r
> Shrink his thin essence like a rivel'd flow'r:
> Or, as Ixion fix'd, the wretch shall feel
> The giddy motion of the whirling Mill,
> In fumes of burning Chocolate shall glow,
> And tremble at the sea that froths below![2]

It is the same with the character of Sporus, a character so detested that detestation acts like an

---

[1] *Mor. Ess.* iv. To Burlington, 119.   [2] ii. 123 ff.

enchantment freeing Pope to squeeze the utmost
sensuous pleasure from its manifestation.

NOTE ON POPE'S HOMER

Pope even goes so far as to 'improve' Homer by
the addition of Ovidian material as well as of the
'Ovidian ornaments' which Warton noted.[1] The
following is the translation of Lang, Leaf, and Myers
for *Iliad*, xxi. 342 ff.:

Thus spake she, and Hephaistos made ready fierce-blazing
fire. First on the plain fire blazed, and burnt the many dead
who lay there thick, slain by Achilles; and all the plain was
parched and the bright water stayed. And as when in late
summer the north wind swiftly parcheth a new watered
orchard, and he that tilleth it is glad, thus was the whole
plain parched, and Hephaistos consumed the dead; then
against the river he turned his gleaming flame. Elms burnt
and willow-trees and tamarisks, and lotos burnt and rush and
galingale, which round the fair streams of the river grew in
multitude. And the eels and fishes beneath the eddies were
afflicted, which through the fair streams tumbled this way
and that, in anguish at the blast of crafty Hephaistos. . . .

Pope translates as follows:

The Pow'r Ignipotent her Word obeys:
Wide o'er the Plain he pours the boundless Blaze;
At once consumes the Dead, and dries the Soil;
And the shrunk Waters in their Chanel boil:
As when Autumnal *Boreas* sweeps the Sky,
And instant, blows the water'd Garden dry:

[1] Joseph Warton, *Essay on the Genius and Writings of Pope*, ed. 1806,
ii. 401 n.

So look'd the Field, so whiten'd was the Ground,
While *Vulcan* breath'd the fiery Blast around.
Swift on the sedgy Reeds the Ruin preys;
Along the Margin winds the running Blaze:
The trees in flaming rows to Ashes turn,
The flow'ry *Lotos*, and the Tam'risk burn,
Broad Elm, and Cypress rising in a Spire;
The wat'ry Willows hiss before the Fire.
Now glow the Waves, the Fishes pant for Breath,
The Eels lie twisting in the Pangs of Death:
Now flounce aloft, now dive the scaly Fry,
Or gasping, turn their Bellies to the Sky. . . .[1]

This illustrates Pope's Ovidian inclination. There is nothing in Homer about the upturned bellies and nothing about them in the Latin and French versions of the *Iliad* which I have consulted. Pope is remembering Ovid's similar description of Phaeton's mishap, when the chariot of the sun, coming too near the earth, dried up the rivers:

> ima petunt pisces, nec se super aequora curvi
> tollere consuetas audent delphines in auras;
> corpora phocarum summo resupina profundo
> exanimata natant . . .[2]

Sandys had translated this by:

> The Fishes to the bottome diue: nor dare
> The sportlesse Dolphins tempt the sultrie Ayre.
> Long boyl'd aliue, the monstrous *Phocae* die,
> And on the brine with turn'd-vp bellies lie.

At this point, however, Pope had an Ovidian precursor among the English translators. Thomas

---

[1] 399 ff.   [2] *Met.* ii. 265 ff.

Hobbes's translation of 1676, which he may or may not have consulted, reads:

> The Eels and Fishes in the water hote
>> Tumbled and turned their bellies up with heat.

The respect for the original Silver Latin epic and for what translators had made and were making of Latin poetry, caused Pope to intensify the pathos of Homer. See, for example, his version of Andromache's lament over Hector's body, xxiv. 906 ff.

INDEX I

POPE'S WORKS

(Unless otherwise stated, the text of the poems quoted is A. W. Ward's in Macmillan's *Globe Library*. Occasional misprints have been corrected.)

INDEX II

SELECTED NAMES OF PERSONS AND WORKS

REPRINTED LITHOGRAPHICALLY IN GREAT BRITAIN
AT THE UNIVERSITY PRESS, OXFORD
BY VIVIAN RIDLER
PRINTER TO THE UNIVERSITY